T0381467

HE MAY NOT COME IN A HURRY, BUT HE ALWAYS COMES IN TIME

DENNY BONNER

WESTBOW
PRESS®
A DIVISION OF THOMAS NELSON
& ZONDERVAN

WestBow Press books may be ordered through booksellers or by contacting:

WestBow Press
A Division of Thomas Nelson & Zondervan
1663 Liberty Drive
Bloomington, IN 47403
www.westbowpress.com
844-714-3454

Scripture quotations marked (NIV) are taken from the Holy Bible, NEW INTERNATIONAL VERSION®, NIV® Copyright © 1973, 1978, 1984, 2011 by Biblica, Inc.® Used by permission. All rights reserved worldwide.

Scripture quotations marked KJV are taken from the King James Version. Public domain.

ISBN: 979-8-3850-3726-1 (sc)
ISBN: 979-8-3850-3727-8 (e)

Library of Congress Control Number: 2024922844

Print information available on the last page.

WestBow Press rev. date: 10/25/2024

CONTENTS

FOREWORD

Even though she was not my actual "birth" mother, I dedicate these lines to the memory of Amanda Francis Bonner Flinders, my paternal grandmother, whom I affectionately grew to know as "Mom." It is a testament to moms and to other people everywhere who have sometimes unconditionally sacrificed nearly everything they had for the welfare of those they loved. Though they may have been insignificant in social stature, wealth, or prominence, they modestly, oftentimes unknowingly and certainly dramatically, impacted future generations by positively changing people's lives as they passionately and deeply loved them. Jesus very clearly expressed this selfless, counter cultural nature of love very plainly in John 15:13 where he proclaimed:

"Greater love hath no man than this: that a man lay down his life for his friends." (KJV)

I sincerely believe that Jesus did not intend, however, for his comments to apply simply to a masculine audience. Women love as well! In fact, I have often experienced that women are perhaps deeper, more intense, and more compassionate lovers than are men. Men tend to be what I sometimes call "Adam's Apple" lovers: specialists at swallowing rather than in publicly and openly shedding tears. They are often hand shakers rather than passionate kissers or huggers. They are often silent rather than outspoken.

I also am not convinced that Jesus intended this revelation to His disciples to apply merely to true, loving friendships. I would further suggest that Jesus was describing the kind of sacrificial, unconditional love that transcends our human capacity to love. The <u>Bible</u> refers to it as Agape love. We cannot genuinely love in this way without God's assistance and grace. With His godly love permeating our hearts, however, we can love others to a superhuman, unimaginable, unprecedented degree. This type of love may not result in death or martyrdom, as it certainly did for Jesus and others, such as disciples Paul or Peter; but it is surely just as godly and heavenly in nature as is any saintly or historic sacrifice.

Mom's life embodied this kind of love. She was not a famous movie star or noted TV celebrity like Meryl Streep or Oprah Winfrey; she never experienced abundant riches or immeasurable wealth as did Leona Helmsley or Christy Walton; she never had an earthly ministry that would equal that of Mother Theresa or Florence Nightingale; and she was never a social mover or shaker. In fact, her entire universe simply encompassed Lewis County and Vanceburg, Kentucky, with a paltry population, at least when I was growing up, of 1,526. She was merely "Mom" to her immediate family, but her Christian influence brightened the lives of nearly everyone she met, particularly those in Lewis County who were fortunate enough to have personally known her. Perhaps you will glean a small sampling of the godly kind of love she emanated from the following pages.

I would also like to dedicate this book to my daughters, Tracey Leigh Bonner and Amanda Jennings Bonner Church, who are the primary sources of inspiration for the writing of these pages. Both of my daughters have been repeatedly amused and fascinated by numerous stories from my childhood experiences and the episodic escapades of my brothers and me as we roamed the rolling hillsides of Lewis County. In a spontaneous and enthusiastic burst of energy several years ago, Tracey impulsively exclaimed, "Dad, you need to write a book about all this stuff. You need to tell your story so others will know who you really are! Perhaps you could inspire others whose plight in life might be like yours!"

Tracey, in fact, was so highly motivated in her commitment to spur me to action that she presented to me a little booklet called *Someday, I'll Ask You* by P. J. Cloud, with which I could chronicle and organize minute details of a life I had often forgotten, except in moments of nostalgia, and begin the process of recollection. That booklet is a simple little journal that asks personal questions about one's life: facts and details that might fade into obscurity or oblivion were they not written down or shared with others. I was not at all convinced, and am still not overly persuaded, that any earth shattering, world shaking, or proverbial comments could issue from the pen of a former bare foot Lewis Country boy who roamed the hills of a 23-acre farm in eastern Kentucky with his two brothers over three quarters of a century ago. Sadly,

I confess, I placed the journal on the shelf to gather dust and to be lost perhaps in oblivion.

Several years later, however, I rediscovered the forgotten booklet, perhaps at the urging of Tracey, wiped off the dust-bunnies and cobwebs, and began the emotional and nostalgic journey through long forgotten but poignant recollections. Even though many of the journal's pages are still blank, thus began my odyssey through latent memories, obscured from proper perspective at the time by the constant trivial struggles and challenges of everyday living. Thanks to you, Amana and Tracey, my "Chocolate Eyes." You were my inspiration.

I would also like to say that one of the most profound lessons I have learned, through both the adversities and sometimes deeply and emotionally poignant moments in my life, is that God infinitely cared for and continues to care for me every day of my life. Psalm 139:13 indicates that he loved and cared for me even before I was born. King David proclaims:

*"You created my inmost being, you knit me together in my mother's womb. I praise you because I am fearfully and wonderfully made." (*NIV)

I am also keenly aware that we often perceive events so differently, both the extremely gut-wrenching traumatic ones and the highly emotionally charged ones, when we view them through the introspective vision provided by intervening years. Events and experiences that once seemed extremely important and significant, when perceived through a more youthful or naïve perspective vision, seem significantly less important with the passing years; and ones we perceived as inconsequential or trivial at a specific moment in time can sometimes assume a more mystical nature than we could have ever imagined when they transpired. This is certainly true as I ponder vague images, remembrances, and reflections forever etched into my subconscious memories.

CHAPTER 1

REFLECTIONS IN THE MIRROR

I Corinthians 13:12: *"Now we see but a poor reflection in the mirror; then we shall see face to face. Now I know in part: then shall I know fully, even as I am fully known."* (NIV)

Perhaps we never fully understand the significance of everyday events in our lives while we are in the process of experiencing them. Perhaps, instead, as we are caught up in the hustle and bustle of everyday life, we spend too many of life's precious allotted minutes pursuing what often becomes meaningless everyday trivia that is too soon forgotten. Perhaps we only superficially glance in the mirror at hazy and vague images that are only a partial reflection of who we really are behind the mirror.

Emily Webb comes to a significant realization in act three of Thornton Wilder's play *Our Town*, when the Stage Manager permits her to return, after her sudden and unexpected death, to relive a very normal day in her life. In emotional retrospection, she suddenly recognizes how very miraculous and profound everyday events really are.

"It goes so fast. We don't have time to look at one another...Do any human beings ever realize life while they live it? Every, every minute?" she very poignantly asks the Stage Manager.

"The saints and poets, maybe-they do some'" the Stage Manager responds.

While some children may possess earlier memories of their childhood experiences than I, the first memory indelibly etched in my subconscious mind is one that perhaps occurred when I was around 24 months of age (At least that is what others have told me, since I was far too young to really understand the full implications of what was happening). The incident probably took place sometime in the middle of December 1944, though my innocent and naive memories do not recall the specific day. I do remember, nonetheless, that this seemingly insignificant day marked a very significant turning point in my life. This was the day Mom providentially appeared in my life, and her house became my home for the next 21 years.

The house where I was born was a small two-bedroom, weather-beaten, gray looking vertical- plank shanty on a small rocky hillside with merely an outhouse, an open well, and no indoor plumbing. It was precariously perched on a small ledge on the morning side of Town Branch Hill Road in Vanceburg, Kentucky, the county seat of Lewis County. Via the winding combination creek graveled, limestone graveled rural road, the route to my birthplace was only about a quarter of a mile "as the crow flies," or at the most half a mile, from Mom's house, just around the bend, but slightly up the hill.

This rustic shanty was also the birthplace of my two brothers: Gary was 16 months older than I, and Jim was nearly two years my junior. I was not old enough to realize the extent of my somewhat rustic existence. Later, as I matured and as my knowledge of the world encompassed more than the boundaries of Vanceburg and Lewis County, I had numerous opportunities to travel; and I became keenly aware that my heritage was truly that of a typically poor "Eastern Kentuckian."

My first memory of my mother, Effie McCleese Bonner, incorporates the resounding thumps of her shoe heels, reverberating on the dilapidated wooden plank flooring of the rustic front porch as she was escorted, head slightly slouched forward, to the Lewis County Sheriff's car that was waiting in the dirt and limestone graveled driveway. I was perched on the front steps, puzzled by the events of the day, certainly lacking a full understanding of the significance of the moment. I do not remember very much about the physical features of her face or of her personal appearance other than the fact that she wore a full-length flowered gingham dress.

Years later, others would remind me that, born in the "hollers of Indian Creek" in rural Lewis County on May 31, 1915, she was a raven-haired beauty with deep, coal black, pensive eyes. She was somewhat coy and demure: a small framed, simple, humble woman who never had much of a chance to experience anything more than an instantaneous or momentary glimpse of happiness during her entire lifetime. In reflection, I often contemplate how sad it must have been that she would never enjoy her three sons' kisses, skinned knees, heroic and epic battles with wild Indians, raging sedge grass fires, snake beatings, or treetop abodes. I was able, after nearly 23 years had passed, however, to establish a somewhat superficial relationship with her; but she never really had a fair chance at being my mother. Her life was destined to be spent in a shadowy alternate reality, and she would pass away of a heart attack in a private care nursing facility in Falmouth, KY, on September 13, 1989.

On this day in December 1944, however, she shuffled past me on the steps, planted a kiss on my forehead, and whispered, "I love you," as deputies somberly whisked her off to the waiting sheriff's car. She certainly knew no more about what was happening than did I, a 24-month-old naïve toddler. Such was the nature of both her innocence and mine.

I do not remember having experienced a great deal of emotional trauma; I do not remember having shed any tears; I do not remember my brothers as having been present; I do not even remember whether my father, Elmer Ray Bonner, witnessed the unfolding events. Time and naiveté erase so many memories! I do NOW know, however, (Perhaps this knowledge was even imparted to me later in life by others.) that this was one of those defining, serendipitous moments which miraculously impact our lives. Particularly when viewed retrospectively, they remind us of God's existence and His loving care for us, even though we may not be wise enough or mature enough to recognize it at a particular moment in time.

"Isaiah" 44:2 tells us not to fear, that God knows us from the womb and is always there to help us:

"This is what the Lord says-he who made you, who formed you in the womb, and who will help you: Do not be afraid..." (NIV)

Miraculously, because of God's infinite love for me and in partial fulfillment of His plan for my life, Mom fully entered my life at this very moment in 1944, changing me forever.

"These three little fellows need some place to stay," she explained to my step-grandfather, Benjamin T. Flinders.

He, of course, hesitated, but graciously agreed; and "Mom," Amanda Francis Bonner Flinders, age 56, became infinitely more than simply a grandmother. She also became my "Mom," mother, father, spiritual mentor, and councilor for nearly thirty years, until her death on March 19, 1974.

My mother, I later learned, suffered from chronic schizophrenia and became a long-term patient/resident at Eastern State Hospital in Lexington, Kentucky. Her residence there would last nearly twenty years. There, she was often heavily drugged, locked in confined quarters, underwent numerous shock treatments, and perpetrated against herself several unsuccessful attempts at suicide, as the scar stretching across her right forehead testified.

The nature of her illness would both taunt and haunt her until her death at age 74. Though she was sometimes temporarily released from Eastern State Hospital to visit for short segments of time, she would live a somewhat vagabond life, moving from one institution or private care environment to another, located in small towns and cities throughout Kentucky, including Lexington, Sanders, Carrolton, Vanceburg, Tollesboro, and Falmouth. Naively, I did not know, at this moment, in December 1944, that she had been mentally committed to Eastern State Hospital. I did not know I would not see her again until nearly 17 years had passed.

It truly was a moment when I could merely glimpse "but a poor reflection in the mirror." I could only know or understand in part. I did not understand that God had miraculously intervened in and positively altered the course of my entire life! When "Mom" intervened in my life, God provided for me a "new" life and a "fresh start" toward becoming what God wanted me to be.

CHAPTER 2

EVERY-DAY, ORDINARY SAINTS

I do not blame God for any of the disappointing events of those first 24 months of my life. Perhaps the chronic alcoholism and frequent roving eye of my father, Elmer Ray Bonner, was a contributing factor. Perhaps my mother's obsessive jealousy and her fits of rage and anger discouraged and drove him away. Perhaps the physical and mental shock of giving birth to three infant boys between April 3, 1941, and June 2, 1944, and caring properly for them was too much for the diminutive, frail body of Effie McCleese Bonner to endure. Whatever the cause might have been, I refuse to believe that the God of ultimate love doles out anyone's life from a stacked deck, nor does he dictate the terms or conditions under which we experience and determine the paths of our lives.

For the most part, our choices determine our destinies: where we go, what we become, and what we do with our lives. While we may certainly inherit those genes that give us the propensity to crave alcohol, we voluntarily choose to yield to the temptations of excessive alcohol consumption. We choose to be angry, mean, and contentious. We choose to have too many children in too short a period, perhaps leading to what today is often termed postpartum depression. We choose not to take advantage of every good opportunity that life presents to us. We choose not to live life to it its fullest extent. We choose to destroy the chances that our children can have normal lives because of our own drug use, loveless marriages, dissention, argumentation, and divorce. We choose to execute and exterminate over 6 million Jews. We choose to destroy lives through perpetual wars, terroristic bombings, firearm assassinations, and other acts of violence. We are often not aware of, during our very limited mortal existence, that God's intent is for us to love each other in obedience to his commands.

I sincerely believe that one of God's primary revelations of His infinite, unfathomable love is through the use other people. Additionally, I believe that many of those people are what Dr. E. Glenn Hinson, former professor of theology at Southern Baptist Seminary, lovingly labeled "everyday ordinary saints." He referred to them as people "scratching around in the sands of your soul." These ordinary saints, sent by God, help us find direction when we stumble around and fall over the adversities of our lives. I believe the Queen of Egypt was an ordinary saint when she tenderly rescued the infant Moses from the bulrushes of the Nile River to enable him to lead the Hebrew people as God intended for him to do. I believe Mother Theresa was an ordinary saint who cared for and loved the sick, the poor, the dying. I believe that that deacon friend who provided spiritual strength and supported me at the time when I most needed him was an ordinary saint. I believe that the doctor who gently prays with his patient before the impending surgery to allay his patient's feelings of doubt, uncertainty, and fragile sense of mortality is an ordinary saint. I too believe "Mom" was my everyday ordinary saint: an angel sent from God at just the precise moment that a disheveled, fragile, and naive 24-month-old toddler and his two brothers needed her. She rescued me from the "bulrushes" of a little wooden shack on a rural hillside in Lewis County and launched me on my personal odyssey to meet God.

Hebrews 13:5 comforts us by letting us know that, at any age, even a naïve, unaware, insecure believer is in God's care:

*"Never will I leave you; never will I forsake you." (*NIV)

From that 1944 December day forward, my life would never be the same. When I join her in heaven, as I am sure I will someday, I want to reaffirm to Mom that she was, and still is, an ordinary saint: my angel and my deliverer.

Dr. Franklin Owen, once retired pastor at Calvary Baptist Church in Lexington, proclaimed a very insightful thought. He said, "You know, sometimes if our good health lasts long enough and if we live long enough, we reach that point where we have more people on this side than we do on the other side." I believe that Mom is truly on the other side.

So, let me be quicky to say that God often sends everyday ordinary saints to us precisely when we most need them. They may not always behave as we would expect saints to behave, but they make those cameo appearances in our lives, and we are forever changed. Our most formidable challenge, in return, is to become every ordinary saints to others as well. We are to demonstrate God's intimate and deeply abiding love to others who are needy or down and out just as they did.

Can any mere mortal ever live up to the principles involved in carrying out that commission? I believe the answer is a resounding, "Yes, with God's help!"

In fact, history, experience, and innumerable saintly/ godly martyrs and commoners from past generations demonstrate to us that He has already done so repeatedly down through history. Those who influenced others were not deluded fools or uneducated oafs. They may have been kings or queens, poets or paupers; but often they were very modest, simple people who simply yielded their lives to the power and leadership of a formidable, loving, omnipotent God.

Furthermore, I confidently proclaim that He will reenact similar events repeatedly down through future generations. We too will have, if we have not already experienced it, the opportunity to change someone's life spiritually and dramatically. That is why God made us a part of His enormous creation.

Exodus 23:20: "*See, I am sending an angel ahead of you to guard you along the way and to bring you to the place I have prepared.*" (NIV)

CHAPTER 3

LONELY PEOPLE

Galatians 6:7-8: "*Do not be deceived: God cannot be mocked. A man reaps what he sows. The one who sows to please his sinful nature, from that nature will reap destruction ....* "(NIV)

After December 1944, my father, Elmer Ray Bonner, yielded his life to alcohol addiction and selected the life of a nomad, wandering from town to town, woman to woman, and bar to bar in search of some semblance of meaning for the rest of his life. Vanceburg became New Albany, Indiana; New Albany became Pittsburgh; Pittsburgh became Massena, NY; Massena became Redding, California; and Redding became Chicago. The cities and scenery changed often, sometimes extending from nearly one coast of the country to the other, but there was never any stability: no lasting peace or happiness for him. Nothing seemed to give his life any real meaning. His labor as a migrant construction worker was always subject to termination because, when he received his paycheck, squandered it in a bar or on another woman in a remote hotel room far from home and showed up

11

for work inebriated, he was inevitably fired and moved to the next town, job, or hotel. Periodically, at the end of his rope and down on his luck, he would return to Vanceburg and Town Branch Hill Road for sanctuary: tearful, penniless, downhearted, and penitent.

"I'm never gonna' drink again!" he would tearfully vow.

Of course, Mom would take him back! After all, he WAS her son! Then the ceremonial cycle would begin anew. I particularly remember one such occasion when he was "down on his luck" as he normally was.

The knock on the front door came, as I recall, sometime around 10:00 p.m. Mom, Jim, Gary, and I had already gone to bed. Since the old white one and one-half story farmhouse was somewhat out in the country, about 1 and 1/2 mile from downtown Vanceburg, we were certainly not accustomed to a knock on the front door at this time of night. There were two distinct knocks and a long pause, followed by three more rapid, aggressive knocks. I did not know, at the time, the secret code that Mom and my dad had devised for her to identify him and for him to gain admittance into the house.

On this occasion, he was on one of his crying drunks, as usual, had lost another job, and had nowhere else to go. He had come for sanctuary to Mom's home on the hill, where Mom would never turn him away, regardless of the circumstances or the time of day or night. He was much like the prodigal son in the New Testament who had squandered his inheritance on indulgent living, discovered himself in some hog pit of life, repented, and returned home to find his father watching and waiting for him to return. If you remember the story of the prodigal son, you will remember the father saw him far off and eagerly ran to greet him, ordered the slaughter of the fattened calf for a reunion feast, then put a ring on his son's finger and a robe around his shoulders, welcoming him with open arms.

Mom did not have a fattened calf, a ring for my dad's finger, or a robe for his shoulders, but there would be a warm bed in which he could sober up and rest for a while until he could get "back on his feet." Tomorrow morning, the aromatic smell of fresh hot coffee, bacon and eggs, and homemade biscuits and gravy would permeate the air, heralding a feast fit for her returning prodigal. He would stay a while, would most likely be stricken by the wanderlust bug again, and venture off to another unknown experience.

For now, however, the anticipatory smells of the regal breakfast yielded to that strange aroma I recall as being associated with my father: a pungent mixture of whiskey, tobacco smoke, and perspiration. The sorrowful prodigal son had returned, and there would be abundant love and compassion from a forgiving mother, at least for the time being.

On one such pilgrimage away from Town Branch Hill Road, my dad would not return; his remains did return, however, for interment at Black Oak Cemetery near Garrison, Kentucky. Perhaps the severity of my mother's emotional illness, the shattered remnants of his broken marriage, the unfilled dreams, or the prospect of rearing three small boys by himself were too much for sobriety. His candle finally burned out in a remote parking lot in

Aurora, Illinois, a suburb of Chicago, on February 11, 1969, only one-month shy of his 55th birthday (March 9, 1914). His wallet and had been stolen, and his identity was unknown for several days before Mom received the dreaded, imminent phone call.

The death certificate listed a heart attack as the cause of death, but I believe his heart had broken or at least begun to atrophy many years prior to that, perhaps on that fateful day in December 1944, when he first wandered away from Camelot. How sad that I have no memories of having spent even one Christmas or Father's Day with my father.

The lyrics of a song entitled "Lonely Voices," written by Billie Hanks, Jr. in 1967, seem always to remind me of my dad:

> "Lonely eyes, I see them in the subway,
> Burdened by the worries of the day;
> Men at leisure, but they're so unhappy,
> Tired of foolish roles they try to play.
> Lonely people do I see,
> Lonely people haunt my memory."

I often wonder how many lonely, disillusioned people pace the busy sidewalks and streets of American cities every day, perhaps amid hundreds, thousands, or even millions of people; yet they experience nothing but lonely, meaningless, unhappy lives. Their fate too will perhaps be excessive alcohol abuse, drug use, or submission to some similar happiness substitute that will result only in more loneliness, discontent, depression, and an eventual premature death, perhaps via a self-inflicted gunshot wound to the temple or a heroin injection directly into the bloodstream. I see lonely people every day. I wonder what their fate will be!

Afterthought:

Despite his loneliness, sinfulness and the resulting depravity in his life, King David expressed rediscovery of hope for his troubled soul in Psalm 40: 1-3.

"I waited patiently for the Lord; he turned to me and heard my cry. He lifted me out of the slimy pit, out of the mud and mire: He set my feet on a rock and gave me a firm place to stand. He put a new song in my mouth, a hymn of praise to our God." (NIV)

God always provides solace and hope for the troubled soul. I wish my dad could have found some such comfort during his abbreviated lifetime!

CHAPTER 4

CAMELOT

Genesis 1:1-3: *"In the begining God created the heavens and the earth. Now the earth was formless and empty, darkness was over the surface of the deep, and the spirit of God was hovering over the waters. And God said, "Let there be light, and there was light."* (NIV)

New light and life came into my world in December 1944. Life with Mom also meant life on the hilly, rock-laden 23-acre farm that my step-grandfather, Benjamin T. Flinders, left to her upon his death from a stroke in 1950. The farm extended from its lower extremities near Town Branch Hill Road on the west, eastward, through three small tobacco fields, to encompass a large, several-tiered, weather-beaten, plank tobacco barn; a concrete, spring-fed watering trough; a rustic weather-stained, coalhouse; and an odoriferous chicken house that reeked with the smell of newly deposited chicken manure. The chicken house, separated into two compartments by a makeshift partition that spanned the entire length of the building, was one of three whitewashed utility buildings that graced the premises. The front compartment, adjacent to the chicken coop, would eventually become the fort where Gary, Jim, and I would fend off the Indian attacks or suffer an assault by wild western ruffians.

When my cousin Rhenda came to visit, cowboy pursuits generally became more domestic in nature, and we often would play "house" in its confines for hours upon hours. During one of our imaginary domestic ventures, "Daddy Ben" playfully married Rhenda and me. I wonder if she ever explained to her husband, Doyle Mills, that he was married to a bigamist and that I had been wedded to her far longer than he had.

When another cousin, Benny Gordon Keairns, arrived from Covington for his two-week visits during the summer months, Rhenda and my marriage often took second place to BB guns and Winston cigarettes, which quickly replaced the grapevine "smokes" my brothers and I had devised.

Located in the very center of this network of buildings was a one and one-half story, white, frame, house that would serve as my home until I went away to Berea College in August of 1961. Two concrete porches ran the length of the entire house. The front porch overlooked the vegetable garden and the tobacco fields. The entire house, perched on the side of the hill, sat amid an elevated clearing that, when you sat in the creaky, chain-suspended swing on the front porch, incorporated the entire valley that melted into the corporate boundaries of Vanceburg with the Ohio River in the distance. At a strategic time of the day, you could hear the shrill whistle of the *George Washington* as it passed, via the Chesapeake and Ohio railroad, through Vanceburg to some distant mythical location such as Cincinnati or Maysville in the west or eastward to South Shore, Ashland, or perhaps even Washington, D.C. You could almost set your watch to 8:00 p.m. when *George Washington* zoomed past the Commercial Hotel on Railroad Street across the tracks from the Vanceburg Depot.

The back porch doubled as a bathroom facility during the summer months. Since there were no indoor plumbing facilities, we were required to "draw" water from the well, heat it on the kitchen stove, pour it into the wash pan on the back porch, and possibly expose ourselves in all our native beauty to anyone who might invade our sacred domain.

The outdoor "facility" was a deluxe model, a weather-beaten, wooden plank "two-holer," that would often accommodate a *Sears and Roebuck Catalogue* or an outdated issue of the weekly *Lewis County Herald* to keep visitors abreast of local and worldly concerns. I guess you could have entertained a guest, if his misery was commiserative with yours, and even have discussed the presidential election at the same time, as you heeded Mother Nature's call.

One of the distinguishing features in the center of the back porch was an underground cellar that, in the earlier days when Daddy Ben was alive, displayed numerous exotic wonders such as long potato bins with rows and rows of freshly dug potatoes, canned corn, beets, or pressure-cooked green beans. Perched atop the cellar was the smoke house, often filled with salt cured country ham, shoulder, or pickled pig's feet. These delights would have provided a more-than-ample feast for the queen and her three young knights. In later years, after Daddy Ben's death, the provisions became scarcer, and the feasts less regal in nature.

Behind the smoke house was an apple orchard, a vast arena of wild sedge grass, and a large, forested area of oak and hickory nut trees that evolved into a thickly overgrown pine grove at the apex of the hill.

I know personally that visitors to this Garden of Eden included Robin Hood and his merry men, Roy Rogers and Gabby Hays, Captain Hook, Superman, Batman and Robin, and even Robinson Crusoe. This rustic paradise was the world we inherited from Daddy Ben.

Many years later, on one of my periodic trips back home, perhaps to attend the funeral of a close friend such as Larry Denham or to work at Baker's Department Store during Christmas vacation, one of the first images I would espy in the distance, when I rounded the bend of Route #9 leading into Vanceburg, was the big white frame house on the hill. There was my Camelot, my sanctuary, my lighthouse, steering me home after a long arduous journey from some distant location. I knew that, when I arrived home, there would be a warm stove, a cup of hot coffee, a steaming hot pot of pinto beans, freshly baked cornbread, a scrumptious homemade apple pie, and, of course, lots of love.

Ironically, the shabby shack where I was born, and that I had occupied as my residency prior to my mother's illness, was visible across the tobacco field about a quarter of a mile from Mom's front porch swing. God not only loves us and provides for our needs; but as comedian and philosopher Bill Cosby poignantly once proclaimed, "God also has a sense of humor."

CHAPTER 5

HE MAY NOT COME IN A HURRY, BUT HE ALWAYS COMES IN TIME

I am convinced that I am a Christian today because of Mom. She was the person who made her three boys attend church services regularly at the Christian Baptist Church on Fairlane Drive in southern Vanceburg. Here, I witnessed evangelists who sometimes leaped over the pulpit and paraded up and down the aisles in their proclamations of the Gospel. I can even remember foot-washing services.

To this day, I do not know whether, or if, the Christian Baptist Church did or continues to embrace denominational ties with the Baptist Church, the Christian Church, or a combination of the two. However, I do know that Mom's faith remained unshaken, even later in life, especially during her declining years when all the rigors of life's adversities began to manifest themselves in her declining health. She lost three children and two husbands to death before her departure to be with the Lord, but her faith grew stronger with each tribulation.

Even when her body suffered the ravages of cancer during the last year of her earthly existence, I can still recall her saying,

> "You know; how could I possibly complain about my life? God has blessed me with a wonderful life. He has allowed me to live in good health throughout most of my life, except for this last year. He has allowed me to live more years than many other people have lived, and, when I look at you three boys (my brothers and me), I realize He has allowed me to have two families, when most people are only allowed one. God has blessed me so much in my life! So, how could I ever complain?"

Her faith was a testament to what Paul proclaims in Romans 5:3-5:

"And not only so, but we glory in tribulations also: knowing that tribulation worketh patience; and patience, experience; and experience, hope: and hope maketh not ashamed; because the love of God is shed abroad in our hearts by the Holy Spirit which is given unto us." (KJV)

What a clear outline of God's process for developing our faith! Tribulation teaches us patience, thus developing a more profound reliance on God during those difficult times. Then, as God shows His persistent, perpetual love through each trial and tribulation, we gain even more experience concerning His presence in our lives.

Ultimately, our hope and faith become stronger with each crisis. We learn that He always has been there and will continue always to be there for us. I am not to the point where I can "glory" in tribulation, as Paul stated, but God surely does use our tribulations to develop our faith.

After Daddy Ben passed away, our financial plight worsened somewhat. He had been the one who tended the livestock and tilled the crops, but this was much more difficult for Mom: a widow with three ravenous grandsons on her hands. When he could stay employed and sober, my dad might send a small check to help care for us, but those meager amounts were very sparse and sporadic. With help from Aunt Boots, we managed to have enough food and clothing; but, for the most part, Mom reared us on the annual income accrued from the small tobacco crop and from Daddy Ben's railroad pension of $69.00 per month. This, Mom acquired at his death after his many years of service as a carpenter for the Chesapeake and Ohio Railroad. Mom had far too much pride and "class" to request "charity," as she called it, in the form of welfare or any other such social service. This was just not acceptable.

This pride was never more visible than it was during her last year on Town Branch Hill Road, as cancer ravaged her body. Since she was too ill to use the outside "facility," the "slop jar," perhaps better known as the "thunder mug," became a necessary inconvenience. Because of the inconvenience and hassle, not only of using, but also of emptying this instrument of necessity, Uncle Bill and Aunt Boots approached her about installing an indoor commode in the front bedroom, where she was sleeping.

Uncle Bill proposed that one corner of the room could be "partitioned off" to serve as needed privacy.

"Mom, we will pay for it," Uncle Bill offered.

"This will be much better for you," Boots surmised. "It will be much more convenient. You won't have to worry about going out in the cold or emptying the slop jar."

"We can install an electric pump and run a water line from the well to the commode," Uncle Bill explained. "I can do most of the work."

"No, I don't want you kids to do that. Why go to the expense and trouble?" Mom countered. "I am doing just fine."

"But, Mom," Uncle Bill began.

"No buts about it!" Mom vehemently proclaimed. "This is how I want it. I have done without an indoor bathroom all my life, so I guess I can do without it now."

Any mention of an indoor bathroom "facility" henceforth ceased to be a part of any future conversation. Mom staunchly defended herself and her ways to the very end. Even when she recognized that cancer was taking its toll on her life, she refused to stay in Mercy Hospital in Portsmouth, Ohio.

"I want to go back to Vanceburg to my home on Town Branch Hill Road!" she adamantly proclaimed. "If I am going to die, I might as well die in my own home overlooking the valley I have loved for so many years. At least I will be in my own bed, not surrounded by impersonal doctors, nurses, and strangers poking and prodding me. I am certainly ready to go, and I know where I am going. I am ready to meet my Lord and savior. So, please, let me die as I want to die."

Uncle Bill and Aunt Boots granted her last wish, and she spent her last few days in the old white house on Town Branch Hill Road in Vanceburg, Kentucky. I believe, even to this day, that there was a certain dignity about her final actions. I have learned to respect her even more during the ensuing years because of who she was and what she believed.

One of the most endearing memories I have of Mom is of her standing at the kitchen sink washing dishes and looking out the window on the hillside images of wild blackberry bushes and tobacco crops, singing "I'll Fly Away" at the top of her lungs. Her faith was the driving force in every chore to which she dedicated herself and in every crisis that seemed to emerge.

Sometimes, I would mistakenly invade her private moments with God and discover her either on her knees praying or reading her Bible, which she did on a regular basis. I fondly remember that, on one such occasion, when the money seemed a little more scarce than usual, she persistently set aside her church offering, not knowing how or when the next bill might need to be paid. She knew God would provide. She confidently proclaimed, "He may not come in a hurry, but He always comes in time."

Surely enough, I witnessed that the money she gave to the church was somehow miraculously restored, almost to the exact dollar amount, later in that same week. He truly did come in time!

Mom was a very skilled seamstress, as well. I recall that if rowdy horseplay resulted in a hole in the knees of my "Billy the Kid" jeans, Mom would cut off the jeans at the knee and hem them with a new seam, making a good pair of blue jean shorts for the summer months. In similar manner, a short sleeve shirt, fit for any boyhood activity, evolved from a long sleeved one with a frayed elbow into a new creation. Because of the social pressures that often accompany school attendance, even for those at Vanceburg Grade School in the 1950's, I remember being embarrassed, on at least one occasion, when some of my unsuspecting classmates were discussing their new Levi Jeans, and I sported only "Billy the Kid" jeans, instead of the more socially acceptable Levis.

Mom was not of an overwhelming physical structure and certainly had little wealth about which to brag, but what a giant faith she had! I hope one day to have as much faith and confidence in God as she had in her little finger. That kind of faith in an "everyday ordinary saint" is what led me to be the Christian I am today. I believe she really did fly away to a "home on high."

CHAPTER 6

PRECIOUS MEMORIES

"Precious memories, how they linger,
How they ever flood my soul.
In the stillness of the midnight,
Precious sacred scenes unfold."

My Aunt Boots' given name was Beulah Marie Bonner, which she retained her entire life. Born March 25, 1909, she was never married. She missed her chance at true wedded bliss when Mom convinced her that, as a young teenager, she was too young to be married; and Boots deferred to Mom's wishes. Otha, the young man who had proposed, eventually married someone else; and 63 years later, after his wife had passed away, he and Aunt Boots reunited. In the intervening years, she had worked at Shelby Shoe Factory in Portsmouth, Ohio, and generally made the trek by Greyhound bus to Vanceburg nearly every weekend, where she would take a taxi to Town Branch Hill Road. She and Otha never married, but during the last three or four years of her life, he treated her like a queen and brought a great deal of comfort and joy into her life. What a wonderful experience it was to witness their fondness for each other for those few precious final years as he catered to her every need. They were like teenagers reliving memories of the senior prom all over again. In case you are wondering about the name "Boots," my Uncle Myron, when he was a mere infant, had a slight lisp and could not pronounce Beulah properly, so it always came out "Boots." The name stuck with her until her death on May 13, 1990.

Even today, many years later, when Christmas arrives at my house, I fondly recall Aunt Boots, Mom, and Christmases spent in the big white house on Town Branch Hill Road. Boots always heralded the arrival of Christmas when the Christmas tree symbolically emerged from the attic and once again became a prominent feature of the living room decor. I say Christmas tree, even though it was miniscule in size; it could not have been more 3 feet tall and had been spray painted a gaudy, silvery white color. Its size limited its capacity to one or two strands of Christmas lights, at the most, but it was ceremonially perched atop the table in the corner of the living room, anxiously awaiting the momentous occasion. The tree was certainly not the equivalent of the Christmas trees that adorn the corridors of Fayette Mall or Macy's Department Store today, but it aptly signified that Christmas was on the way for three expectant, mischievous, wide-eyed impish boys on Town Branch Hill Road in Vanceburg, KY. When Mom finally placed the nut bowl on the coffee table and filled it with English Walnuts, we knew that Christmas was not far away. All we had to do was wait for the highly anticipated moment on Christmas Eve when

Aunt Eula, Uncle Bill, and my cousin Rhenda would close Our Kay's Grill and join us for the opening of the Christmas packages.

Mom and my younger brother Jim always slept in the upstairs room adjacent to where Gary and I slept, except when Boots came home for the weekend. Jim was then uprooted from his bed and would sleep with either Boots or Mom temporarily. One of the annual rituals involved our pre-Christmas visit to Boot's bed. Early on an eagerly anticipated morning, we three boys would invade Boots' bed with excitement and glee as we bombarded her with questions. All three of us would pile on the bed around her, and the conversation would begin.

"Boots, let's talk about Christmas."

"What would you boys like for Christmas?" she playfully teased, trying to elicit a response.

"I think I'd like a pair of gloves," I began.

"What kind? Wool gloves, leather gloves, or just plain work gloves?" she further questioned.

"I think I'd like a pair of leather gloves. You know the kind that has a wool lining?"

"Yes, I've seen those at Baker's Department Store," she responded. "Is that all you want Santa to bring you?"

"No, there are some other things I'd like, but that is the top thing on my list," I suggested, not wanting to close the door on receiving and even greater bounty from Santa. I would then begin to share my Christmas list, sometimes suggesting a Roy Rogers double holster cap gun set, a set of warm earmuffs for school, a Lone Ranger air rifle, or perhaps a pair of "slip-over" boots or galoshes for the trek home from school on a frigid winter day.

Each of us would continue to suggest what we would like to have for Christmas until we had exhausted all the possibilities. Generally, Boots was the one who made Christmas happen at our house because she had the steady job and would ensure that our Christmas fantasies were not disappointing.

Additionally, my Uncle Myron and his family, including his wife Marie and his two children, Mike and Debbie, would also be home, waiting for Christmas Eve. Uncle Myron would secretly don the Santa Claus suit, appear miraculously outside the dining room window, trudge in from the cold, wintery night, and dole out the presents, hopefully, without igniting the Santa Claus beard with his cigar. My cousin Burgess (Rival Burgess Walters) assumed the awesome task of holding the reindeer at bay under the old hickory nut tree at the end of the gravel driveway until Santa could return for them. Sometimes, Rhenda or Gary, in fear of Santa Claus, would scream, run, and hide hysterically behind the kitchen stove at Santa's first appearance. Uncle Bill and Uncle Myron might playfully engage with each other in a wrestling match on the dining room floor to see who could "best" the other after Uncle Myron had returned from playing Santa Claus.

Eventually, however, the excitement of the evening wore down, and the frivolity ended with three "droopy eyed" boys being whisked off to bed, even though they were reluctant to miss anything else the grownup world might include. They would fight sleep until the droopy eyes could endure no more and would finally succumb to "visions of sugar plums" that might include the savory aroma of tomorrow's feast of baked turkey, mashed potatoes, dressing, green beans, and homemade pumpkin pie. Christmas was a memorable and joyful time at our house, even though the money was sometimes in short supply. Generally, all the family members joined in and made it work.

Another excitement that accompanied looking forward to Christmas was the abundance of Yuletide activities at The Christian Baptist Church, about a mile from our house by foot, via Fairlane Drive, in the south end of Vanceburg. My brothers and I were not particularly fond of the journey by foot, especially during the cold and snowy winter months. Sometimes, a church member gave us a ride, but we could not always count on this luxury. Most of the time, we were required to make the walk, sometimes twice each Sunday.

Very seldom did Mom allow us to miss Sunday school and church. Generally, she would give each of us a nickel as a Sunday school offering. Sadly, we would often squander our offering at the grocery store two doors down from the church on a package of Lays Potato Chips, Wrigley's Juicy Fruit, or Spearmint gum prior to Sunday school. We naively believed that she was unaware of our escapades, but I feel sure she knew all about them. I discovered in later years that many of our best-kept secrets were not all that secret after all. She knew most of them, but never revealed such knowledge to us.

Annually, during the Christmas season, Santa Claus would make an appearance at The Christian Baptist Church, and we all paraded down to the front of the church to receive our Christmas treat bags. The gift consisted of a simple brown sandwich bag with all sorts of pleasantries such as an apple, an orange, some Juicy Fruit gum, some chocolate candy, several pieces of assorted hard candy, a candy cane, and other assorted goodies. How amazing that a simple brown bag could generate such joy and jubilation! To us, it began a week of some serious sugar overload. Among my favorites were the gummy orange slices that somehow miraculously attached themselves to the hard candy in the bag, forming a sticky, gooey, glob that inevitably resulted in sticky fingers and messy mouths for all of us. That made little difference, however. Had the goodies arrived in a golden treasure chest, we could not have been more elated.

Before the Christmas bags were distributed, many of the children of the church participated in the annual Christmas program under the direction of Sister Katie Pilot. This program generally consisted of having each child parade across the stage, climb atop a stool or chair so that he/she was visible over the railing that surrounded the pulpit, and recite his/her two or three line memorized "piece" to the congregation. One of the most embarrassing moments of my entire life occurred during one of these performances.

I proudly walked across the stage to take my appointed place, tripped over the electrical cord attached to the Christmas tree at the back of the stage, and toppled the entire Christmas tree onto the stage amid the laughter of everyone in the entire congregation. Mom, however, was still proud of me, despite the erupting chaos, and even complimented me on how well I had recited my "piece." She was ever the encourager, except when we became too boisterous or unruly during the church service. Then, if needed, she would give us the Amanda Francis Flinders stare (Move over Tubby Smith.) and clear her throat loudly enough for the entire congregation to hear. All the attention would turn to us.

Uncle Bill was on call, if needed, to be her enforcer. Sometimes, Mom even gave us the opportunity to select our own means of punishment from the limbs of the shrubbery bushes surrounding the front porch. She instructed us to strip away the leaves, once we had selected the intended instrument of punishment, and we experienced several swats across the back. Psychologists might label this as child abuse today and would probably even question its necessity, but I believe I am a better person because of it. As far as I know, I have not suffered any permanent physical or psychological repercussions. I only know that my love for Mom and the disciplines she taught me has increased during the passing years, especially after having two daughters of my own.

CHAPTER 7

PETTICOAT JUNCTION

Uncle Bill and Aunt Eula were always very special members of our family. Uncle Bill served as Vanceburg's only mail carrier for as long as I could remember, at least while I was in school. Aunt Eula, at Our Kaye's Grill Restaurant and Bus Station, served up the best open-faced roast beef sandwich I had ever savored while Uncle Bill was busy delivering the mail. As mentioned in the previous chapter, Uncle Bill was also the "enforcer" for Mom: called into duty and service if Mom needed a heavy masculine influence to assist her in enforcing strict disciplinary measures on her three mischievous and sometimes wayward musketeers.

Meanwhile, Aunt Eula was always eager to enlist me for service at Our Kaye's Grill: washing dishes, chipping ice, or, especially during the peak dinner hours, serving tables. Chipping ice was a rather demanding chore since it required walking nearly a quarter-mile round trip to Gale Denham's Locker Plant on the east side of the Lewis County Courthouse to obtain the seemingly gigantic chunk of ice. Then, I lugged a 25-pound block of ice to the rear entrance of Our Kaye's Grill, and laboriously chipped the ice into small pieces that could have been enjoyed by a king as easily as by prominent Vanceburg business executives such as Tater Lykins, Ralph Davis Senior, Cecil Baker, or Floyd Voiers. The meager wages from such chores allowed me to participate in several games of billiards at Gardner Rowe's Billiard Emporium, listen to Elvis' latest hit 45 rpm record on the Juke Box at Sullivan's Drug Store, or secretly purchase a 20-cent package of menthol flavored Winston cigarettes, as I yielded to sinful living.

Six days my senior, their only daughter, Rhenda Kaye Bonner, was a very special cousin and friend. She was born on July 31, 1942, and my birth followed just six days later, August 6, 1942. She was also the namesake for Our Kaye's Grill and Restaurant. We grew up together, romped and cavorted on the hillsides of Lewis County together, played house together, conducted pet funerals together, worked at the restaurant together, attended both public school and college together, celebrated Thanksgiving together, and experienced Christmas together for over 70 years. Ours was truly a lifetime experience together. I still miss my composite "wife," sister, and dear friend almost daily.

Uncle Bill and Aunt Eula were always doing good deeds for others, sometimes at great personal expense and sacrifice to themselves. This was particularly apparent when the court granted them legal custody of four small children in 1964.

In May of 1964, Aunt Eula's sister, Juanita Blankenship, was shot to death in the front doorway of her small home on Front Street in Vanceburg. Her five small children were eyewitnesses to the event, perpetrated by the woman who, at the time, was having an extra-marital affair with their estranged father Ralph Blankenship. Since the children had to have a place to stay, Aunt Eula and Uncle Bill, one month later June 19, 1964, assumed custody of all three girls: Teresa, age 11; Rebecca, age 8; and Boni, age 7. They would obtain legal guardianship for the children in May 1965 and would rear and care for the three girls until they left home for college: all four of the younger children, in fact, had an opportunity to attend college under the tutelage of Uncle Bill and Aunt Eula. Dane, only 6 years old when his mother died, went to live with his father in Campton, Ky., along with his older brother Tommy.

The home of Aunt Eula and Uncle Bill at 201 West Second Street in Vanceburg became the home, not only of Rhenda Kaye, their own daughter, but also of the three small, adopted Blankenship girls. I have often pondered the thought that Aunt Eula and Uncle Bill were also among the everyday ordinary saints referred to by E. Glenn Hinson. They rescued and saved those children, just as Mom had rescued my two brothers and me 21 years earlier. Their entire lives focused on rearing the three small, adopted girls and their own daughter, nourishing all of them to adulthood. Aunt Eula and Uncle Bill loved them as their own children, taught them about God at Vanceburg United Methodist Church, and nurtured them as only God could have given them the strength and monetary resources to do so.

Jeremiah 17: 7–8: *"But blessed is the man who trusts in the Lord, whose is in him. He will be like a tree planted by the water that sends out its roots by the stream. It does not fear when the heat comes; its leaves are always green. It has no worries in a year of drought and never fails to bear fruit."* (NIV)

Uncle Bill and Aunt Eula were "trees planted by the water," more everyday ordinary saints, and certainly bore fruit for the heavenly father. They became a refuge for God's children of misfortune and made a sustained effort toward turning these precious, precarious, sometimes precocious lives, into God directed, meaningful, and productive ones.

Uncle Bill was the only male presence in the home, so he aptly and lovingly proclaimed his home "Petticoat Junction." I am sure there was an abundance of stockings, ladies' underwear, curlers, and lipstick. Perhaps he experienced the same threats and challenges that I did as the father of my own two daughters and the only male in an otherwise all-female world. Perhaps he speculated, just as I once humorously mused, that his means of death would be strangulation via the panty hose draped across nearly every available bracket in the bathroom.

Aunt Eula and Uncle Bill both experienced horrible deaths within two weeks of each other in December 1995. Aunt Eula passed away on December 5, 1995, after an extended painful battle with cancer, and Uncle Bill suffered instantaneous death via a gunshot wound to the left temple at the hands of a carjacker on December 16, 1995, after the perpetrator commandeered Rhenda and Doyle Mills' car in the Frankfort Walmart parking lot. Rhenda tragically lost both her parents, not only within two weeks of each other, but also within two weeks of Christmas in 1995.

CHAPTER 8

POPS

Rival Burgess Walters, born on January 13, 1925, was the "cosmopolitan" member of the family. The son of Lora Walters, who later married Arthur Jahn, Burgess never really knew his father, Fister Walters. When he was a mere infant, his father abandoned him and moved away from home. Consequently, Burgess was almost single handedly reared by his mother. When the opportunity presented itself, he moved away from Vanceburg to Dayton, Ohio, and then to New York City, where he spent most of his adult life.

At first, he worked as an instructor at Arthur Murray Dance Studio in NYC, but he then attended Cornell University and became a renowned cosmetologist in some of the most exclusive salons in NY, including the one in the lobby of the Essex House Hotel, overlooking Central Park. Because of his alternate sexual preferences, he became somewhat the black sheep of the family at a time in history when the alternate gay lifestyle could not be commonly accepted in the culturally conservative social circles of Vanceburg. In NYC, however, he could melt into the impersonal crowds that paced the streets of NYC, and he was free to live his life as he wanted, far from the confines of his naïve rustic Lewis County heritage. He often bragged about and displayed signed photographs of some of his most prominent clients: people such as Ann Miller, Fred Astaire, and Liz Taylor. He apparently was a very sought-after hairdresser in NYC and could blend into the cosmopolitan atmosphere without a great deal of judgment about his private life, even during the time when a homosexual lifestyle was not as commonly accepted as it is today.

On his infrequent visits to Vanceburg when I was a teenager, we would sit at Mom's kitchen table and converse for hours about New York City, my future, and the people he had met. When I became a disk jockey and news reporter for the local radio station, WKKS, his discussion would focus on my career plans and where I might attend college. Sometimes, his visit would coincide with our summer vacation from school, and he would borrow Uncle Bill's dilapidated Nash Rambler to take us to the Old Ford swimming hole on Kinniconnick Creek. His summer visits always included scheduling our much-dreaded visits to the office of Clem Hill, the only dentist in Vanceburg. Of course, he always paid the dental bill.

Sometimes, he would desire a little more "action" than what the Vanceburg culture could provide, and we would secretly make the nearly 30-mile trip to visit the Pine Bar in Portsmouth, Ohio. Here, together, we could savor the pleasures of fresh draft beer and enjoy the country music sounds of the local entertainment.

Mom would have killed him had she suspected where he had taken us. I believe, in retrospect, however, that he recognized the void left in our lives when our own father left home and that he sought to be a substitute father for the three of us as best he could.

After Donna and I married, especially when our daughters came into the family, he began the tradition of annual visits to our home on Maywick Drive in Lexington, either at Thanksgiving or Christmas. His visits became a part of an annual ritualistic escape from the tedium and impersonal atmosphere of New York and a return to some semblance of a warm, normal, everyday life far from metropolitan crowds and traffic congestion that were so customary in a teeming metropolitan atmosphere. With us, he could sit in front of a roaring fire in the family room and read a book to Tracey, proudly and ceremoniously present Amanda with an excessively riveted Miss Piggy blue jeans vest, feel a sense of family identity, and avoid judgment in any form. He always knew he had a place to call home where he could be accepted and still be himself.

Perhaps this is why, at his death of a heart attack on August 16, 1988, he named me as his only heir, leaving all his personal property to me in his will. He considered me his son. In fact, his friends in New York City believed I really was his son. He would proudly display to them any Christmas card or Father's Day card endorsed to "Pops," as he preferred me to address him when I was in high school.

My family in Lexington gave him a place of refuge and acceptance that he could experience nowhere else, so I really *was* the closest thing to a son he would ever know. I feel honored to have known him.

God wants us to love everyone without judgment or prejudice.

Paul clearly delineates this standard for God's love in I Corinthians, Chapter 13, better known as the "Love Chapter" in the New Testament. Verses 4-13:

"Love is patient, love is kind. It does not envy, it does not boast, it is not proud. It is not rude, it is not self-seeking, it is not easily angered, it keeps no record of wrongs. Love does not delight in evil but rejoices with the truth. It always protects, always trusts, always hopes, always perseveres. Love never fails . . . And now these three remain: faith, hope and love. But the greatest of these is love."(NIV)

How much different the world would be if we could all honestly and sincerely practice this kind of love in all our human relationships. Divorce, murder, jealousy, racism, sexual prejudices, discrimination, and yes, even the most brutal wars would perhaps cease to exist.

CHAPTER 9

METAMORPHOSIS

Webster's Collegiate Dictionary defines metamorphosis in the following manner:

> "A passing from one shape or form to another: complete transformation of character, purposes, circumstances, etc: a developmental change in form, structure, or function in an organism."

My brothers and I were always very inquisitive in our explorations of the rustic hillside behind our home on Town Branch Hill Road in Vanceburg, and, on one of our outings, we discovered a cocoon delicately and mysteriously attached, hanging precariously, to one of the wild saplings that had invaded our domain. Mom explained that, even though it appeared to be very ugly, its true nature and inherent beauty were very deceptive: that it would, in fact, develop into something very beautiful: a butterfly. That thought captured my imagination, so I eagerly treasured it and eventually asked Mrs. Voiers, my

4th grade teacher at Vanceburg Independent Grade School, about it. Thus began my introduction to metamorphosis, as she thoroughly explained the mysterious process.

I proudly displayed the cocoon in a place of prominence on the back porch and, during the next several weeks, witnessed one of God's most wonderful miracles as the intriguing item of interest became the focal emphasis of my scientific exploration. Eventually, its grotesqueness was replaced by unimaginable beauty that would perhaps capture the exuberance and imagination of some curly, golden haired young miss as she innocently scampered through a valley of daffodils and daisies, and it soared away from me into a brilliant light blue summer sky to claim its destiny as one of God's most beautiful creatures.

On December 2010, Donna and I chanced to discover that we also unknowingly possessed an item of great value and beauty, even though it had been discarded for several years as merely nothing but rubbish.

When my cousin Burgess passed away, he appointed me as the sole executor and only designated heir of his entire estate. Uncle Bill and I, subsequently, made the pilgrimage to his apartment at Waverly Place in New York City; sorted through his personal property and belongings; and, in the spring of 1999, arranged for Mayflower Moving and Storage Company to transport his furniture to a storage facility on Old Frankfort Pike in Lexington. Some items were disposed of in a garage/yard sale, some were bestowed as remembrance gifts to other family members, and some were designated to suffer their ignoble destiny as refuse in the local Bluegrass Landfill near Tollesboro, KY. Still other items, however, those we deemed as having enough value, we retained. The grungy looking secretary with the glass doors, foldable green velvet covered writing surface, and broken leg was displayed in our living room; and the decrepit settee became a resident of our outside backyard storage shed for the next eleven years.

In the fall of 2010, on a whim, Donna and I decided to check on the possibility of restoring the settee as our mutual Christmas gift to each other. Perhaps it had some value, we reasoned, and might be worth restoration, even though one of the arms had been totally broken off and rested apart from the entire unit atop the metal worktable in one corner of the storage shed. Someone had removed the springs and created a makeshift plywood base that had been screwed onto the frame to support the flat, floppy cushions. By the time we decided to retrieve it from the shed, the cushions were rotten, moldy, and dust covered with several years of accumulated storage cobwebs, dead insect remains, and debris. It was a wobbly mess and did not seem to be a much of a positive prospect for future use.

Nevertheless, we laboriously heaved it onto the pickup truck, threw the missing arm and floppy cushions on top of it, and hauled the remains to Morningside Woodcrafters, Inc. at 718 National Avenue in Lexington.

"We have an old settee that we would like for you to check out," Donna explained. "We would like to know if it has any value and whether or not it would be worth restoring."

"Let me take a look at it," he responded, as the sawdust covered, middle-aged man followed us to the truck.

"Boy, it sure is a mess," he responded casually, as he

mounted the truck bed to peruse the victim of many years of neglect. "Let's move it inside where I can get a better look."

Once we were inside, he subjected our victim to a more complete inspection.

"This, in its day, would have been a very valuable piece of furniture," he proclaimed. "Did you notice the decorative inlaid pattern in the wooden back of the structure? That is a very distinctive pattern that, along with the highly ornate wooden structure and elaborate craftsmanship, make what would have been a very nice piece of furniture."

"I know it is in very bad condition," Donna acknowledged. "How much do you think it would be worth if it were totally restored to its original condition?"

"Oh, I would say somewhere between $6,000 and $8,000," he responded. "It would have been a top of the line, very valuable pieces of furniture during its time."

Donna was flabbergasted.

"Is it realistic thinking to have it totally restored," she asked, "or would it be cost prohibitive?"

"Well, we would have to glue it back together, reattach the arm, remove the plywood cushion base, install new springs, and refinish the entire thing," he responded.

"How much would it cost to do all of that?" Donna asked.

"Well, I think we could totally restore it to its original condition for around $625," he responded. "Now, we do not do upholstery, so you would have to take it somewhere else to get that done."

Our Christmas gift to each other was agreed upon,

and today, we possess a very valuable fully restored settee as the centerpiece of our living room furniture. In addition, we were so impressed with their work, that we employed the same company to refinish and restore the three-legged secretary. It is now valued at $4,500-$5,000. Who would have ever believed that two castaway pieces of junk furniture, restored, would be worth an estimated combined value of $10,500 to perhaps as much as $13,000?

This was truly metamorphosis at work. Something old and decrepit was transformed into something of beauty and great value.

Recently, during my morning walk around the neighborhood, a profound, spiritual thought suddenly dawned upon me. Isn't this what God does to people? He is the master of metamorphosis. He changes people from trash to treasure, from worthless to worthy, from pitiable to pious, from vain to valuable, and from decrepit to deified. The pages of history and the Bible are replete with examples of ordinary people who have been changed in such a way.

Dan Cooper, who was my pastor most of the time when I was a member of Calvary Baptist Church, once delivered a very powerful children's sermon. He presented the idea to the children that when you become Christians, God comes and dwells inside you. I can almost still envision that little hand going up in the air saying, "How can God live inside me when I am so small, and he is so big."

Pastor Dan's comment was, "Well He may stick out some, but don't you think that's what Jesus wants? Doesn't

Jesus want to stick out in us so that other people can see Jesus in us."

It's true, God wants to stick out in all of us fellow Christians!

★★★NOTE: Chapter 35 delves into the subject of how God transforms and uses the metamorphosed lives of everyday human beings to accomplish His will.

CHAPTER 10

THE WATERING TROUGH ESCAPADE

Job 1:21: *Naked I came from my mother's womb, and naked I will depart.* (NIV)

Having had children of my own and having experienced the challenges of rearing two daughters, I cannot imagine what Mom and Daddy Ben must have endured when they took the three of us into their home on Town Branch Hill Road. Imagine for a moment what it would be like to be in your mid 50's and to assume the almost singular responsibilities that would accompany the rearing of three very young, impetuous, and rambunctious boys on a 23-acre hillside farm in Lewis County. Even more challenging, imagine that, five years later, you are a 61-year-old widow who, almost entirely on your own, must discipline, train, provide for three boys, and navigate them safely through the preteen and teenage years. My brothers and I as teenagers did not make it any easier.

Our escapades included smoking grapevine cigarettes, parachuting from the top of the tobacco barn with feed sack parachutes, making roaring campfires, and sometimes igniting the sedge grass on the entire hillside. Occasionally, we would torture one of the cats by rubbing his backside with corncobs and then dousing his posterior in rubbing alcohol. We dared to imitate Batman by attempting to fly, with feed sack capes, from the lofty heights of the front porch roof. We erected tree houses that were architectural masterpieces and often witnessed their collapse as we tumbled headlong to the ground in an avalanche of rope, saplings, and twigs. We killed blacksnakes, hung them in trees, and beat them with sticks until there was nothing left except a few stringy stands of snakeskin suspended from the tree. We even discovered that cow patties made great frisbees, long before we experienced the joy of real frisbees for the first time. Sometimes our naiveté placed us in perilous situations, as when we ventured to navigate the broad expanse to the raging Ohio River during the spring flooding season in a makeshift canoe constructed of plywood. Miraculously, we survived all our adventures with only minimal scaring, despite our sometimes-outrageous flirtations with danger and death. We were even among the first people to streak, long before it became a popular fad. In fact, we did not even know what streaking was.

There were two water sources on the farm. One was a "dug" well which served as our primary water supply. Mounted on the top of the wooden platform which served as a cap for this well was a bright red manual water pump, the shaft of which extended perhaps ten or fifteen feet to the bottom of the actual well. The long-arched handle extended away from the pump, and after priming the pump, we could draw the water needed for bathing, drinking, or cooking. Changing the water quite frequently, however, became a necessity because some form of iron contamination very heavily adulterated the water. The result was that, after it had set for any extended period, rusty brownish sediment would collect in the bottom of whatever container was in use. The water would then assume a very stale "tinny" taste. To my knowledge, Mom never conducted any tests to determine the suitability of the water for human consumption. This was, however, the primary source of my drinking water for nearly nineteen years, and it served to remove the mud, filth, and grime during my bathing sessions on the back porch after a day of chasing Indians or burying a deceased family pet after we had conducted a graveside church service.

The other, shallower well, about twenty feet from the house on the southern side of the back porch, was not really a well because its source was a natural water vein that oozed from the hillside into a manmade makeshift cavern. It was capped and funneled into an underground water pipe, which, in turn, supplied water for the six by two-foot concrete watering trough, about twenty-five feet down the hill. This watering trough had been constructed by Daddy Ben to water the livestock: a horse, two cows for fresh milk and butter (except when the cows had eaten green onions), and a multitude of chickens to supply an ample abundance of eggs for the morning breakfast. This watering trough provided a means for the Bonner boys to initiate their naval assaults on Nazi Germany, or sometimes it would be used to launch the baking soda powered nuclear submarine or frogman that had been procured from the cellophane prize envelope of a Cracker Jack, Cheerios, or Corn Flakes box. This watering trough was the site of the infamous streaking episode.

"Shine" Burris, one of Daddy Ben's numerous friends, came to visit us one day. I do not remember why he was there. Perhaps he had come to obtain a gallon of fresh milk, or perhaps he came to procure a pound of Mom's recently churned butter.

More likely, he came to savor one of Daddy Ben's bottles of homemade grape wine. I do not remember why his name was "Shine," though I am sure there is a wonderful story behind that name since moonshine bootleg whiskey was a common commodity around Vanceburg. The only thing I know for sure about him was that he was from a nearby town we knew as Black Oak, Kentucky, a tiny community of several families about four or six miles east of the Vanceburg city limits on Route 8, which ran somewhat parallel to the Ohio River.

I also remember that he was quite a jokester, always telling a funny joke or inciting some innocent tyke to perpetrate an act of mischievousness. On this occasion, he innocently, or perhaps not so innocently, commented on the watering trough.

"Man, that is a nice watering trough," he stated.

"Have you boys ever gone swimming in it?" he asked teasingly.

"No, we play in it all the time, but we've never gone swimming in it," Gary responded.

"Well, you boys need to go swimming in this fine watering trough." he jokingly asserted

"Well, we've thought about it some," Jim announced.

Shine had planted the seeds of temptation, and the prospect of having our own private swimming pool was certainly enticing.

After Shine was long gone, the hills echoed with joyous giggles as three totally naked, lily-white torsos with deeply tanned faces, legs, and arms streaked from behind the white-washed coal house to claim the watering trough for their initial baptism into their Town Branch Hill Road, Lewis County, Kentucky, iron-contaminated swimming hole. It was an exhilarating experience!

Jesus words concerning baptism by the Holy Spirit recalled by the apostle Paul in Acts 11:16 states:

> *John baptized with water, but you will be baptized with the Holy Spirit.* (NIV)

We were not participants in baptism by the Holy Spirit, but good old Lewis County iron contaminated spring water served as an appropriate substitute for our initial baptism.

CHAPTER 11

MICKEY MOUSE AND REPENTANCE

2 Corinthians 7:10: *Godly sorrow brings repentance that leads to salvation and leaves no regret, . . .* (NIV)

I first yielded to criminal activity and a violation of the law when I was in Mrs. Beavers fifth grade class at Vanceburg Independent Grade School located on West Second Street on the banks of the Ohio River near where Salt Lick Creek emptied into the wide expanse of the Ohio River. I do not remember with certainty whose property I coveted, but I believe that the victim of my crime was Ruth Ann Stafford, and I know she would forgive my confession, even after the passage of over 70 years.

The object of my affection was a Mickey Mouse wristwatch. I did not have the luxury or financial resources to own any wristwatch, much less a very special Mickey Mouse watch. I distinctly recall that this one featured the face of Mickey Mouse with one outstretched arm of Mickey serving as the minute hand and the other arm sufficing as the hour hand. Thus, by reading the position of the arms, one could determine the time of the day.

I vividly remember plotting the dastardly and diabolical deed for several weeks before I perpetrated the actual crime. I charted the watch's activity, and noticed the occasions on which Ruth Ann wore it, when she removed it, when she used it to calculate the time of day, and where she discreetly secured it in the book compartment of her desk during recess. I waited and schemed, and finally the opportunity arose.

Mrs. Beavers had asked me to stay behind for a few minutes while the other students streamed forth to savor the allurements of the swings and sliding board adjacent to the eastern exterior entrance of Vanceburg Independent Grade School. I do not recall what she had asked me to do, but I do remember that we finished whatever task it was, and she then went out to the playground to supervise the other students, leaving me behind for just enough time to accomplish my goal.

I obtained the item of my fancy and secured it within the safe confines of my book satchel where no one would be able to see it. The heinous crime had been committed! With great exhilaration, I exited the building to join the other students on the playground. Now I simply had to live with the pangs of guilt that would accompany the event.

When everyone returned to class from recess, Ruth Ann did not immediately notice the missing watch. In fact, it did not become the object of discussion until school dismissed at the end of the day, and all of us began to assemble our books, papers, pencils, and crayons. Then the ensuing questions erupted:

"Who would have done such a thing?"

"When would he (In those days we would not have worried about gender.) have had an opportunity to do it?"

"Weren't all of us together for the entire day?"

"Wasn't Mrs. Beavers always with us?"

"Don't we all trust each other?"

"We all know each other, and surely none of us would have done it. Right?"

I kept silent, but my conscience began to gnaw at me, condemning me for what I had done. The ethics and morality of Amanda Francis Flinders had "kicked in."

Since Vanceburg Independent Grade School could not afford the luxury of school buses, Gary, Jim, and I, along with several other students, generally made the trek home in groups via Fairlane Drive to our homes in south Vanceburg. Sometimes, my brothers and I rode to or from school with Don Burton, our neighbor, who lived directly across the street from us on Town Branch Hill Road.

On this occasion, a nearly one and one-quarter mile walk gave me lots of time to think about what I had done.

"What would all my friends think if they knew about this?"

"What would Ruth Ann have to say?"

"What could I say to her?"

"What could I say to other class members?"

"What would happen if Mom found out?"

"Even worse, what if Uncle Bill found out?"

"Would Vanceburg's only police officer, Earl Billman, arrest me?"

"Would I be put in jail?"

"What could I do, now that the crime had been committed?"

"Everyone in Vanceburg (all 1,526 people) would know what I had done."

By the time my brothers and I had dropped off several classmates and had walked the seemingly interminable odyssey to Morgan Skagg's Grocery at the corner of Fairlane Drive and Town Branch Hill Road, I had devised a plan.

Town Branch Hill Road changed to Mud Alley when it intersected Fairlane Drive, and on the opposite side of Mud Alley from Skagg's Grocery, on the corner next to the Vanceburg Supply Lumber Company facing Fairlane Drive, was a row of makeshift mailboxes. Two fence posts driven into the ground, a weather beaten 2 X 6 board securely nailed to the two posts, and several galvanized metal mailboxes aligned along the length of the edifice graced the awaiting mail outpost. Tall, imposing weeds surrounded the structure, except where the tires of the mail carrier vehicle had carved out deep ruts as it approached the mailboxes for its daily deliveries. Over the years, several layers of litter had accumulated in the weeds surrounding the mailboxes.

"This is a very good location." I surmised.

When Jim, Gary, and I arrived at the intersection of Fairlane Drive and Mud Alley, just as we were crossing Fairlane Drive to begin our walk up Town Branch Hill Road, I discreetly wandered alone into the vicinity of the mailboxes.

Would you believe I MYSTERIOUSLY "found"

a Mickey Mouse watch in the debris surrounding the mailboxes?

"Could this be the wristwatch that disappeared at school on that very day? I could return it to its rightful owner."

Miraculously, I was a 5th grade hero of magnificent proportions the next day at Vanceburg Elementary Grade School. Nobody ever knew, until now, what Paul Harvey would call "the rest of the story."

Mom, if she had known, would probably have rebuked me by citing scripture, perhaps Proverbs

11:19: *The truly righteous man attains life, but he who pursues evil goes to his death.* (NIV)

CHAPTER 12

A TIDBIT OF AFRICAN AMERICAN FOLKLORE

Psalm 57:7: *My heart is steadfast, O God. My heart is steadfast: I will sing and make music. Awake, my soul! Awake, harp and lyre! I will awaken the dawn.* (NIV)

It seems that music has been an integral part of my entire life. When we were growing up in Vanceburg, my brothers and I infamously, perhaps even notoriously, were dubbed "The Bonner Boys." We three comprised a very good sounding vocal trio, at least in our minds. We sang for an occasional talent show, or at a special event, but we often simply sang hymns for the Christian Baptist Church, where Mom was a member, or at Vanceburg United Methodist Church, where Uncle Bill, Aunt Eula, and my cousin Rhenda attended. We frequented the Methodist church more often when we were teenagers because more young people our age attended there, including many of our friends from Lewis County High School. After church, many of us would assemble at Bill Sullivan's Drug Store to listen to the juke box belt out

Elvis Presley's "Blue Suede Shoes," Bill Haley's "Rock Around the Clock," or some other rock-n-roll favorite. Sullivan's Drug Store was also a very good place to hang out for another reason we could savor the luxury of a greasy hamburger, French fries, and a fountain Coke for a mere 75 cents.

Sometimes our singing resulted in a talent show competition and required a road trip to some exotic long-distance location, at least for us, such at Portsmouth, Ohio, or Maysville, Kentucky. We never really won very many contests, but we did enjoy the experience of singing together most of the time.

I guess I must have had a somewhat decent singing voice because teachers frequently invited me to sing at school for my classmates or at some other special social event. When I was in fifth grade, for example, I was even able to experience the distinct pleasure of being invited back to sing for a group of captivated fourth grade students.

On one memorable occasion, when I was in the sixth grade, the leaders of the PTA even invited me to sing *"De* Blue Tail Fly,**"** perhaps better known as "Jimmy Crack Corn," at the annual spring PTA meeting.

In case you are not acquainted with "De Blue Tail Fly," as popularly recorded by the late Burl Ives and apparently written by an author who remains anonymous to this day, it was passed down to future generations through oral tradition, as noted by some historians, and is alleged to have been among Abraham Lincoln's favorite songs.

It was a typical "black faced minstrel" song, written

somewhere around 1844-1846, perhaps as a black slave's lament over the untimely and tragic death of his white taskmaster. The last several verses detail how the master's horse, perhaps due to the slave's negligence, is bitten by the blue tail fly and resorts to a frantic bucking and kicking maneuver, resulting in the master's death. However, the general belief is that the writer may have been rejoicing over his cruel master's death and may have even deliberately contributed, through negligence, to his master's actual demise. Subsequently, the writer perhaps facetiously attributes the master's death to the blue tail fly, masking his chicanery and jubilation.

The big moment had finally arrived. Gleefully and proudly, I took my place on the sixth-grade stage to share with my peers and their parents my PTA rendition of "De Blue Tail Fly." I apparently did a masterful job with the first few verses, finally arriving at the climactic final verse:

De pony run, he jump, an' pitch,
An' tumble massa in de ditch.
He died, an' de jury wondered why.
De verdic was de blue tail fly.

This was the precise moment of what my friend Earl Reum, a noted humorous and motivational speaker from Denver, Colorado, might refer to as "the single, most significant learning experience of my life." My nervousness resulted in a slight slip of the tongue, and the word "pitch" did not come out the way it was supposed to (Use your imagination to determine what the uttered word might have been).

Also imagine the humiliation and ensuing laughter as the revised lyrics wafted through the hallways of Vanceburg Grade School to resound for all posterity and the metropolitan Vanceburg community to hear. I am sure I did, as the psalmist at the beginning of this chapter affirmed of music, "...waken the dawn," though maybe not in the way I had intended.

CHAPTER 13

MUD, MANURE, AND MOTHER NATURE

For as long as I could remember, Mom always had some livestock around the barnyard on Town Branch Hill Road: chickens, pigs, milk cows, and even some ducks. They provided fresh meat and poultry and dairy products to supplement the canned green beans, corn, and potatoes that often populated the shelves of the cellar behind the back porch during the frigid winter months. Mom frequently recruited her three boys to deliver homemade churned butter or fresh cow's milk to neighbors and friends who had become our normal customers. I am sure the Lewis County Health Department would have frowned upon our business ventures had they known about them, but this was a good source of supplemental income if times really got rough; and we were too naïve to recognize that we were in violation of multiple laws governing safe health regulations. In the spring, the abundant crop of wild green onions that grew in and around the fields and pastures often adulterated the milk resulting in a taste and that made it almost impossible for human consumption. If you have never savored the rank odor or taste of milk contaminated by green onions, you have certainly missed one of life's most "interesting" challenges.

At that time, a single lane, approximately 30 feet long, creek graveled driveway provided access to our 23-acre farm from Town Branch Hill Road. The driveway, separated by a gate and wire fence from the actual barn yard, led directly into the weather beaten sliding double doors of a gigantic barn, which consisted of four separate stalls for housing, feeding, and milking the cows in the sometimes-brutal winter months. In the fall, after the tobacco crop had been suckered, topped, cut, and harvested, the tiers and rafters of the barn provided ample space for protecting the tobacco from the elements until it came "in case" and was ready for stripping and the ensuing trip to Farmer's Tobacco Warehouse in Maysville, Ky.

The previously mentioned barnyard adorned the front of the actual edifice, separated from the garden and tobacco fields by means of a sagging dilapidated woven wire fence. Toward the east and slightly up a gently sloped incline, the barnyard incorporated the previously mentioned watering trough at the upper end of its boundaries. A rusty metal-hinged latched gate, adjacent to the watering trough, separated the barnyard from the actual front lawn of the white two-story framed house that served as my home during most of my childhood and teenage years.

To obtain entry to the main driveway, we were required to open the gate at the western corner of the yard and walk perhaps three-hundred feet through the barnyard to the longer, horizontal gate that separated the driveway from the barnyard. In the winter, this became extremely difficult to navigate because, as the cows travelled back and forth between the barn and the watering trough, the entire area became an almost impassible quagmire of water, mud, and cow manure. The topography, made more complicated by the overflow from the watering trough and the slightly sloped terrain that spanned the entire expanse from the watering trough to the barn, often became a sloppy mess. One was required to gently and cautiously "tip toe" through the entire area to navigate the treacherous path, especially in the winter months.

On one occasion, "Mother Nature" had provided an ample abundance of rain for several days.

The Bonner Boys had applied to sing in another regional talent show in Portsmouth, Ohio. Sue Plummer, a very talented local singer, would travel with us and sing her rendition of "Blue Moon." Uncle Bill, as I recall, was to pick us up at our home on Town Branch Hill Road and provide the transportation to and from Portsmouth. All the preparations and rehearsals were completed, and we three boys were ready to discover our destiny as the next preeminent gospel music trio.

We had attended several invitational gospel music events in the Lewis County High School gym, which annually hosted a gospel music festival/jamboree by inviting gospel music groups from surrounding counties and towns. That gym served as the only facility of any size within the immediate vicinity of Vanceburg that could host the local Lewis County High School Lions basketball games, the high school junior-senior prom, and the annual Lion's Club Talent Show, as well as the Minstrel show.

Perhaps we aspired to be the next gospel music trio that might rival in skill such well known groups as The Chuckwagon Gang, The Blackwood Brothers Quartet, or The Statesmen's Quartet: all of which were very popular both locally and nationally at the time. At any rate, our appointed time with destiny had arrived. We were to travel to Portsmouth, Ohio, for competition in our premier, big time, talent show.

I must have been the last one to make the hazardous trek to Uncle Bill's old dilapidated 1950 Nash Sedan, because, as I recall, everyone else, including both my brothers, sheltered from the downpour, were already positioned in the back seat for the odyssey via Route #8 through Black Oak, Garrison, Quincy, Firebrick, and South Portsmouth to Portsmouth, Ohio. I apparently forgot something and had to retrace my steps through the treacherous quagmire back to the house and then discreetly sidestep the cow manure and mud on the return odyssey through the barnyard.

I had navigated about half the distance on the return to the car, when a deluge began, as suddenly the intensity of rain dramatically increased. Realizing that, if I dallied, I was going to become soaking wet, I dramatically increased the intensity of my efforts until I was in a desperate run to try to avoid the downpour. I managed to navigate the overflow ditch from the old concrete watering trough and speedily approached the sprawling hickory nut tree that marked the midway point, the point of no return, between the house and the barn. I do not vividly recall all the gory details, but I do remember slipping on one of the protruding roots of the hickory nut tree, losing my footing, and desperately trying to regain my footing, as I went sprawling through the mélange, one of Mother Nature's best concoctions. You can imagine the image I projected: a white sport coat, black slacks, a black bow tie, and a gruesome mixture of mud and greenish brown cow manure. I was a sight to see!

History does repeat itself, however! Several years later, this adventure was duplicated, perhaps even topped, by my daughter Amanda on the playground of James Lane Allen Elementary School in Lexington. She recreated the entire event when she slipped and went sprawling into a mud puddle during recess and emerged encased in mud. In fact, the teachers who were supervising could not even recognize her. Her face, eyes, and ears, totally encrusted in mud, concealed her identity! It was not until they took her in the building and washed her face that they discovered this was Amanda Bonner. Like father, like daughter! The only difference was that, for her, there was no cow manure.

Psalm 40:2: *He lifted me out of the slimy pit, out of the mud and mire: he set my feet on a rock and gave me a firm place to stand.* (NIV)

CHAPTER 14

BEELZEBUB

We three Bonner boys did not always have the best or latest style of clothing, nor did we experience all the amenities that our fellow classmates did. Though Mom and Boots adequately provided for our basic needs, perhaps the desire for the "finer things" in life, such things as Lays Potato Chips or Pepsi Colas, is what prompted our youthful and naïve encounter with interior forces, sometimes evil, that exist deep down inside the human psyche.

Gary, Jim, and I devised a plan that we, since we had not been able to relish the pleasures of a Pepsi Cola for an extended period, would take all the appropriate actions to ensure that we could savor the delights of this delectable delicacy. This event occurred in the days when all soft drink bottles were made of glass, and a deposit was subsequently required on each purchase so that retailers could be sure the bottles were returned for proper sterilization and recycling. The empty bottles could then be "cashed in." This meant that their value could deducted from the next purchase of the same soft drink product. We knew that Mom kept the empty Pepsi bottles in the cellar adjacent to the back porch under the smokehouse, so our plan was to obtain enough empty bottles to secure our purchase and to make the pilgrimage to Morgan Skaggs' Grocery Store at the bottom of the winding hill where Town Branch Hill Road intersected with Fairlane Drive. We reasoned that one cannot steal from his own parent. Mom would certainly understand that it was simply borrowing! The three of us would share the Pepsi equally.

We secretly invaded the damp confines of the underground cellar, obtained our desired treasure, stealthily sneaked our way past the huge oak tree in the front yard, and scampered down the creek graveled wheel ruts of Town Branch Hill Road. There were two nearly ninety-degree curves in the road that led the way to Morgan Skaggs' Grocery, but we quickly mastered the curves and the jagged gravel that lined the road, finally arriving at our predetermined destination. We collected the deposit on the bottles, purchased the Pepsi, and embarked on the seemingly successful and uneventful return journey.

We were of such a young age that I do not remember how the order of the participants was determined, but I was the first person to get my swig from the Pepsi, Jim was the second, and Gary was the third. I do remember very vividly, however, that, when Gary received his opportunity to partake of the forbidden fruit, his share of the bounty appeared to be much less than what both Jim and I had received.

"You drank too much!" he screamed at Jim. "You got more than your share."

"I did not!" Jim responded

"Yes, you did!" Gary retorted.

"No, I didn't." Jim defended himself.

"I said you did!" Gary shouted.

"And I said I didn't!" Jim exclaimed

The ensuing argument rapidly escalated and climaxed with Gary's angry response, "I'm going to kill you!"

He picked up a stone about the size of my fist and hurled it toward Jim, who, by this time, was speeding up Town Branch Hill Road to escape the attacking aggressor, kicking up dust and gravel as he went. The rock found its intended target. Jim collapsed in the middle of the road, and blood began to mingle with the dust as it streamed from the gaping wound in the back of his head.

"Oh, I've killed him!" an immediately penitent Gary hysterically screamed. "I'm sorry. I didn't really mean it."

Meanwhile, the prostrate victim lay suspiciously inert in the middle of the road.

Jim was not seriously injured, and he did survive the assault. However, that episode could have resulted in an entirely different outcome which could have been shockingly irreversible.

Was Gary angry enough, at that specific moment, to kill his brother? Did he really, with malice, intend to injure his younger brother when he picked up the rock and hurled it toward his fleeing victim? What would have been the repercussions had he killed his own brother? Obviously, Gary would have experienced a great deal of instantaneous remorse, but he would have already unknowingly perpetrated an incident that could have perhaps haunted him for the remainder of his life. Even worse, as remorseful as he might have been, there would have been no way to undo the damage!

What makes us respond this way in a moment of rage and anger? Was this how Cain responded in anger to his brother Abel in "Genesis" 4:2-8? Was this how Cain perhaps experienced similar remorse at the death of his own brother, once he had committed the horrible act.

Perhaps the apostle Paul captured the essence of this spontaneous and uncontrollable thinking in Romans 7: 15-21, when he said:

I do not understand what I do. For what I want to do I do not do, but what I hate to do . . . As it is, it is no longer I myself who do it, but it is the sin living in me... I have the desire to do what is good, but I cannot carry it out. For I do not do the good I want to do, but the evil I do not want to do-this I keep on doing. Now if I do what I do not want to do, it is no longer I who do it, but it is sin living in me that does it. So . . . Although I want to do good, evil is right there with me. (NIV)

I believe, as did Paul, that the struggle between good and evil (God and Satan) is a perpetual daily challenge throughout our entire lives. It has become so apparent in some of the heinous murders that have been perpetrated against fellow human beings.

I personally experienced this struggle when I was tempted to shake my own infant daughter because of her excessive crying, not realizing that shaken infant syndrome is a major factor in child abuse, often resulting in serious brain damage or even death. I once lashed out to my wife in anger, saying things I should not have said, only to later regret them. I have slammed my fist through an uncooperative closet door and had to justify my antics to an unsympathetic doctor who, nevertheless, expected me to forfeit the fee for my indiscretion. I have had to explain to a curious mechanic how a "stubborn" lawn mower suffered extensive damage from a barrage of hammer blows at the hands of a frustrated, angry perpetrator.

Many years later, while teaching *Lord of the Flies* to a class of high school students at Lafayette Senior High School, William Golding again reminded me of this human struggle. The boys in Golding's narrative had to attempt to justify their violent actions against each other in the same manner. Isolated from the confines and restraints of any adult civilized society when they were stranded on a remote isolated island, did they intentionally kill Piggy, as well as both the boy "with the birthmark" and Simon? As their entire society on the isolated island unraveled, and rules and regulations were no longer in effect, were they deliberately intending to kill Ralph and mount his head on the stake in the middle of the forest, treating him in the same way they had treated the wild boar earlier in the story? Even more challenging, was the behavior of the adult rescuing military officials, who were stalking their own adult enemy, any more civilized than that of "savage" uncivilized youth stranded on a remote, uncivilized island in the middle of some unknown ocean? After all, the adults were seeking to kill their prey as well. Golding refers to this "inner enemy" in *Lord of the Flies* as "Beelzebub," another name for Satan.

I believe the apostle Paul would have agreed with Golding's conclusion.

Perhaps this inner struggle and momentary impulse explains why my brother's response, "I'm sorry. I really didn't mean it!" has haunted and intrigued me down through the years. Despite the truth that Gary deeply loved Jim, I believe that, at that one precise moment in time, because of his anger, he meant to harm Jim. A moment later, however, he would have regretted it for the rest of his life.

This is how Satan sometimes controls our lives. He takes advantage of our unpredictable and spontaneous nature to trap and ensnare us. We just must hope that, in our "precise moments," we have not already done something that is forever irreversible and damaging.

Even if the irreversible were to happen, however, God still offers grace and forgiveness. We are not necessarily destined to spend our entire lives with deep guilt complexes and unresolved psychological baggage. King David exemplified this forgiveness in the Bible when he asked forgiveness for his sin.

Psalm 40:1-3: *I waited patiently for the Lord: He lifted me out of the slimy pit, out of the mud and mire: He set my feet on a rock, and gave me a firm place to stand, He put a new song in my mouth, a hymn of praise to God.* (NIV)

Though the causes of David's distress in this prayerful psalm are not specifically stated, perhaps he uttered these words after he had deliberately sent Bathsheba's husband into imminent death in battle to cover up his adulterous act with her. He, consequently, had suffered the depression, shame, humiliation, and punishment that had accompanied his sinful act. In his time of utter despair, he had sought forgiveness from God, and God lovingly forgave him and restored peace to his penitent heart. What a testament to God's boundless love!

There is still hope when we trip, fall, and discover ourselves at "rock bottom." We may have temporarily, and even unknowingly, yielded in weakness to the influence of Beelzebub (Lord of the Flies), but God still offers forgiveness, restoration, and peace.

CHAPTER 15

LOVE AT FIRST ~~SIGHT~~ (FIGHT)

As I explained in one of my previous chapters, my brothers and I sometimes had to walk to our home on Town Branch Road via Fairlane Drive (US 59). Joyce Silvey, one of my classmates in both Vanceburg Grade School and Lewis County High School, lived at 703 Fairlane Drive about two blocks north of the Morgan Skaggs' Grocery.

I fell madly in love with Joyce Silvey in the seventh grade. Unfortunately, it was an unrequited love: she, in fact, never knew I was in love with her. Sometimes, on the walk home from school, as I meandered by her house, particularly if I were alone, I would very casually cross to her side of the road long before I got there to see if I could get a fleeting glimpse of her. Perhaps you can recall when you were a seventh grader in love for the first time! You had to be cool and inconspicuous. Certainly, the secret object of your affection should not be cognizant of your obvious flirtations.

Sometimes, I would deliberately slow almost to a crawl so that I could spend as much time as possible lingering in front of her house, casually sneaking discreet glances over my shoulder until I was either out of sight or could no longer endure the pain of my over-the-shoulder flirtatious endeavors. Sometimes, I would drop the contents of my school bag, dispersing them all over the coarsely blacktopped two-lane highway so that I would have to pause in front of her house and slowly regroup my possessions. To my knowledge, she ever noticed me on any of those occasions. However, Richard Sexton somehow became aware of my infatuation with her.

Later, when we were in high school, Richard, "Mickey" Dunaway, and I became very close friends. Mickey had his driver's license and a car, so the three of us did nearly everything together. We double dated, sometimes triple-dated together, slipped into the drive-in theater in the trunk of Mickey's car, and shared many meals at each other's homes. The three of us even opened our own private poolroom on the opposite side of Harper Street in a dilapidated vacant building, just behind Richard's house.

In grade school, however, Richard and I were not close friends, and a seventh-grade secret love triangle resulted in a serious love confrontation between the two of us. Neither Richard nor I had ever had a date with her. Who, in fact, is really going to have a serious date in seventh grade? Richard somehow discovered that I had a romantic interest in Joyce. Since he liked her also, it was not acceptable that I should express any interest in her. Richard had to defend his manly territory and sought me out on the playground of Vanceburg Grade School beside the swing set.

"Have you been flirting with Joyce Silvey?" he asked.

"Yes, I have," I confessed.

"Well, I don't like it when someone flirts with my girl!" Richard aggressively proclaimed.

"I didn't know she was your girl," I innocently explained, "and I didn't know you had been going out with her."

"I haven't been going out with her," he confessed, "but she is my girl!"

"She can't be your girl if you haven't been going out with her," I countered. "Besides, I can flirt with whoever I want to."

"I'll show you who you can't flirt with!" Richard belted out.

He suddenly lunged for me, and before I knew it, we were in a full-fledged fight to the finish. We were slugging it out pretty good. I felt his fists pelting my face; and more in defense than anything else, I reached for his throat, clenched my hands around his neck, and began to choke with all my might.

It worked. His eyes were protruding from his swollen, scarlet face, he was gasping for air, and his hands were desperately attempting to wrench free from my grasp. I had won!

At that precise moment, I experienced perhaps one of the most foolish moments of my life.

"I don't want to kill him." I remember thinking. "Maybe I should let up."

Against my better judgment, I did release my grasp, and Richard Sexton proceeded to beat me to a pulp! So much for letting one's conscience get the best of him!

Later, when we became good friends, Richard and I were able to joke about the silliness of two seventh grade secret lovers fighting over a girl they had never dated.

Proverbs 17:14: *Starting a quarrel is like breaching a dam: so drop the matter before a dispute breaks out.* (NIV)

CHAPTER 16

A BASKETBALL JERSEY FIASCO

I was not a very good athlete when I was a student at Lewis County High School. I did play little league baseball during the summer months on the baseball field behind the old Lewis County High School on Fairland Drive, but my real love was always basketball, even though I was not very good at playing the game. During my freshman and sophomore years, the basketball season opened with a great deal of expectation. Generally, everyone would have to buy a new jock strap, some gym shorts, and a pair of white high-top Tony Taylor Converse basketball shoes. The highlight of the opening of the season would be when the coach assigned playing squad jerseys with the players' numbers on them. Those of us who were less gifted athletes were only subordinates: we did not receive numbered jerseys since there were not enough for the entire basketball squad, especially if the number of players on the team exceeded 10. Instead, we scrubs suffered the humiliation of wearing simple white tee shirts if we were sitting on the bench. If we were fortunate enough to receive our summons to enter the game, we would strip off our white tee shirts, toss them behind the bench, and check in at the scorer's table to enter the game. We simply had to wait for the player who was exiting the game to report to the sidelines. He, in turn, would have to strip off his numbered jersey, toss it in our direction, and don his white tee shirt when he took his place on the bench. You can imagine the excitement and thrill of pulling someone's cold sweat drenched jersey over your head to enter the game: a humiliation we were willing to suffer simply to get into the game. Finally, we would realize our big opportunity to achieve athletic prominence and notoriety.

We had plenty of time to think while we were sitting on the bench. Generally, my thoughts centered on how our coach, Bob Wright, had severely misjudged my talent and how much I could significantly contribute to the team if I were only given the opportunity.

"He just doesn't know how good I really am," I would surmise. "If he did know the extent of my talent, I would be a starter."

On more than one occasion, I imagined how I would win the game for the Lewis County Lions:

> "There are only 3 seconds to go in the game. The score is tied 65 to 65 in the regional championship game. The ball comes to Bonner. He takes a long shot from beyond the circle. The fans rise to their feet as the ball arches interminably toward the rim. The ball seems to be in

slow motion as it begins its decent toward the basket. The fans erupt in a burst of spontaneous energy and excitement! The Intense anticipation rises to a fever pitch! SWISH! Nothing but net! The avalanche of fans victoriously storms center court in ecstasy and carries Bonner from the floor on their shoulders, as the visiting team melts into oblivion and humiliating defeat!"

"Can you believe it?" the public address announcer screams to the frantic crowd, now rushing center court. "Lewis County has won the regional championship for the first time in 40 years. Denny Bonner has come off the bench and carried the Lewis County Lions to the state tournament on a last second shot!"

I rehearsed the scenario a thousand times in my imagination. In fact, on this day, I was so caught up in my reverie that I did not hear Coach Wright call my name. "Bonner, go in the game for Joe Bud Staggs. He needs a rest."

"I am actually going into a game!" I exclaimed to myself in disbelief. "I am finally going to get my chance to prove to everyone what I really can do."

I raced numbly to the scorer's table, uttered, "Denny Bonner for Joe Bud Staggs," sat on the floor in front of the scorer's table and waited for a break in the game.

Finally, the play on the court ceased, Joe Bud rushed to the sidelines, ripped off his jersey, and threw it in my direction. My brain might as well have been a blob of

Jell-O. I had no idea about what I was doing. I nervously grabbed the jersey, excitedly pulled it over my head, and rushed the court expectantly to claim my destiny.

Just as I had anticipated in my imagination numerous times, I stole the ball from the opposing guard on the next possession and rushed toward the goal for my dramatic layup: my moment of destiny. The crowd rose to its feet in anticipation and, laughing hysterically, cheered me on in my All- American endeavor. I rushed to the basket and lightly banked the ball into the basket. The crowd, now whipped into frenzy, was laughing and cheering wildly. It took a few minutes for me to realize why.

In the excitement of entering the game and having my opportunity to gain fame and fortune, I had not realized that I had put my head through one of the armholes and my left arm through the head hole in the jersey. As I rushed to the basket in anticipation of my glory, I was surely a glorious sight! Furthermore, my moment of fame, very short lived, as I soon discovered, became even more humiliating. I had scored a goal in the wrong basket and had scored two points for the opposing team. My opportunity at legendary fame and glory quickly metamorphosed into one of my life's most embarrassing moments.

Hebrews 12:1: *Therefore, since we are surrounded by such a great cloud of witnesses, let us throw off everything that hinders and the sin that so easily entangles, and let us run with perseverance the race marked out for us.* (NIV)

I ran the race with perseverance and had a great cloud of witnesses; I just put my head in the wrong opening and scored a basket for the wrong team.

CHAPTER 17

HIGH SCHOOL SHENANIGANS

At the risk of sounding slightly conceited, I must confess that I was a very good student when I was in high school. I made very good grades; but, at the same time, I was somewhat of a smart aleck in the sense that I could make good grades and still be mischievous. In the ensuing years, when I became a high school language arts teacher at Lafayette High School in Lexington, I would encounter several students who were very much like me. They would always be up to some kind of trouble but would be given a great deal of leniency because they were always very good students. These are sometimes a teacher's worst nightmare because you never know what they are going to do. They are always plotting some classroom prank, but they are beyond reproach academically. What can you do with such a student?

On the Thursday before Memorial Day in 1958, when I was a sophomore at Lewis County High School, my mischievousness finally caught up with me. I do not recall specifically who else was involved, but I believe

Mickey Dunnaway and Richard Sexton were the two other culprits.

Since I always made good grades and was generally on the honor roll that was published in the weekly newspaper, the *Lewis County Herald*, I also always seemed to have a great deal of leisure time during the last week of school. Generally, I was exempt from taking all my final exams in my classes. This meant that somehow those of us who were not taking final exams had to entertain ourselves in some way or be entertained and supervised by a teacher who was not giving an exam at that time. Oftentimes, Bob Wright, our athletic teacher and basketball coach, assumed that responsibility. Bob was a wonderful basketball coach, who later moved to Ashland, Kentucky, to become basketball coach there and coached the Ashland Tomcats to a state basketball championship in 1961. One of his prize players on that team was Larry Conley, who later played guard for Adolph Rupp's team, affectionately known as Rupp's Runts.

During the last week of school, which spanned Memorial Day weekend in May 1958, I was exempt from all my final exams, so I spent almost the entire week playing softball under the supervision of Bob Wright.

We three soon tired of softball, so we devised a plan to avenge the perceived antics of our *General Business* teacher, John Spriggs. We considered Mr. Spriggs to be somewhat of a smart aleck teacher because he was always making some snide remark or joke about something that happened in class, sometimes at an expense to our fragile egos. In retrospect, I am now aware of the fact that he tried to use humor to keep the attention of his students, much as I did, in my own way, when I later became a teacher. I perhaps always seemed rebellious when he reminded us to keep our fingers on the home keys and not to hunt and peck. I reasoned that if God had wanted the pinkie finger to reach the outer extremities of the top row of keys, He would have made that pinkie finger longer. So, the three of us concocted our scheme to get even with Mr. Spriggs.

Our principal at the time was Teddy Applegate, also a frequent victim of pranks by a group of students who generally arrived early in the morning before many of the teachers had arrived. Teddy was of an average height with a double chin and rather rotund appearance. His physical appearance prompted the definition of "abdomen" in the annual yearbook one year as, "The thing that keeps Teddy Applegate from seeing his feet."

One student periodically set fire to the hallway trashcans, requiring an early morning evacuation of the building. She even unscrewed the dome part of the bell that signaled the beginning and end of classes and threw it in the rising backwater of Salt Lick Creek and the Ohio River that often invaded the high school premises during the spring rainy season. Sometimes, the backwater would back up into the bathrooms and drains, and we would get an unexpected vacation until the water had subsided.

It was hilarious to witness Teddy Applegate as he hustled up and down the hallway blowing an athletic whistle to indicate the end or the beginning of another class period.

During the winter months, Teddy habitually checked the thermostat before the beginning of each day to be sure the temperature setting was adequate. That thermostat controlled the heat for the entire high school building and was located on the right-side wall of the old creaky gym that then served as the study hall. The elevated stage at the northernmost end of the gym housed the high school library. It became a common practice for someone to hold a lighted match under the thermostat just before Teddy had a chance to check it, elevating the temperature to an unbelievable level.

"Whew, it is very hot in here!" Teddy would proclaim as he turned down the thermostat. Later it would have to be adjusted again as everybody began to freeze to death.

But, getting back to my story, Mr. Spriggs was the very proud owner of a brand-new solid black Volkswagen Beetle. In those days, I believed all VW Beetles were black. I had never previously seen one, of course, so they had to be black. I am not even sure how Mr. Spriggs even acquired a VW Beetle in Vanceburg, Kentucky.

If you know anything at all about a VW Beetle, you know that the exhaust system consists of two tiny "pea shooter" tailpipes that protrude from under the rear mounted 4-cylinder engine. Students were always doing something to abuse Mr. Sprigg's VW Beetle. Sometimes it would end up on the front sidewalk of the school or on the top of the pitcher's mound on the baseball field; and, on at least one occasion, it even made an unexpected, miraculous appearance in the center aisle of the gym/ study hall.

This VW Beetle became the target of Denny Bonner, Mickey Dunaway, and Richard Sexton, the Thursday prior to Memorial Day in May of 1958. Our plan was very simple, but not intended to be vandalistic in nature. We would sneak off from the softball game and stuff paper in the two tailpipes protruding from the rear of the vehicle. We gathered our supplies and sneaked around the building to assault our intended victim. One person was to keep an abundant flow of supplies to the other two. I was one of the "stuffers." Since I do not remember who the other "stuffer" was, I am going to say it was Richard.

"Mickey, you wad up the paper and hand it to us. Richard, you take the left tailpipe, and I'll take the right one."

We diligently began our work.

Suddenly, "What do you boys think you are doing?" abruptly interrupted our intense concentration on the imminent task. It was the voice of our principal, Teddy Applegate.

We had been so busy laboriously completing our dastardly deed that we had not even noticed him when he stepped around the corner.

"Well, Sir, we noticed that somebody had stuffed Mr. Spriggs' tailpipes with paper, and we were simply trying to remove it," I ventured with as much innocence as I could muster.

"Yes, we were just trying to help," explained Mickey.

"Yeah, we just found it when we were passing," Richard added.

Teddy did not buy our explanation. "You boys need to come into my office," he proclaimed in a very threatening manner.

So, the three of us were taken into Teddy's office and individually questioned about our intended motives.

Richard was first, Mickey was second, and I was last. I had time to do a lot of thinking while I was waiting. My turn finally came.

"Don't you know you could have done a lot of damage?" Teddy prodded. "If you had put that paper in too tightly, you could have damaged the valves to his engine and caused his engine to burn up," he explained. "That would have been a major expense. How would you have paid for the damage?"

"I didn't think about that," I uttered, and then realized that perhaps I had accidentally confessed to the crime.

"I ought to get that paddle and give you a big thrashing." He exclaimed. "What would your Uncle Bill say?"

His hand reached for my head in a feeble attempt to grab my hair, but his hand kept sliding off. Thanks to an abundant supply of pinkish Butch Wax on my flattop haircut, his hand could not establish a firm grip. I was safe from a hair pulling.

"You are suspended for the rest of the school year, and I will withhold all your grades for this year. That means you will have to repeat your sophomore year!" he announced.

I was devastated! My entire sophomore year was lost. I numbly left his office and began the seemingly interminable trek out Fairlane Drive to Mom's house, where I would have to explain my early dismissal from school to her. My Aunt Boots was there for the Memorial Day weekend, as was Uncle Myron and his entire family. I would be an embarrassment for the entire family. In fact, everyone in Vanceburg would know.

"What are you doing home?" Mom asked. "Why are you home from school so early?"

"I got in trouble at school, and I have been suspended for the rest of the year," I explained.

"Are you serious? What did you do?" Boots joined in the conversation.

"Well two friends and I discovered some paper stuffed in Mr. Spriggs' tailpipes, and we were trying to get it out, and Mr. Applegate caught us and thought we put it in there, and I have been suspended from school for the rest of the year," I innocently explained. "Mr. Applegate even told me he would not give me my grades for this year."

"He can't do that!" Uncle Myron came to my defense. "He can't take away your grades."

Now, here, I must suspend my story to tell you a little about my Uncle Myron. He was an imposing man of about 6 feet and 5 inches and nearly 250 pounds. He had enlisted at an early age, against Mom's wishes, into the Marine Corp as a 17-year-old and had served in the Pacific Campaign during World War II. In fact, he suffered several battle wounds during his stint in the Marines and possessed two Purple Hearts for his heroic service. He was not a man to mess with! In addition, he possessed a strong affinity for beer and bourbon. If he had had more than one should normally drink, he was very difficult to have to confront or control. His face would redden, and he would start telling suggestive, off-color jokes to anyone in earshot, embarrassing both Mom and his wife Marie. I remember one Thanksgiving when, slightly inebriated, he grabbed the turkey from Mom, spread its wings, and flew it all over the house.

Mom, however, would not let him bring alcohol, even beer into the house, so, when he visited us on the hill, he had to make frequent trips to the trunk of his car to get enough refreshment to change any setting into a party atmosphere. On this Memorial Day weekend in 1958, Uncle Myron was "ripe."

"Mr. Applegate even tried to pull my hair," I explained, "but his hand kept slipping off."

"Where are my car keys? I'll go whip up on him!" Uncle Myron headed for the kitchen door.

"Now, Myron, don't get so upset." Mom pleaded. "You have been drinking, so please stop and think a moment. Don't rush off and do something you may later regret."

"No. I'm going to whip up on him! He can't pull nobody's hair. I'll show him!" He opened the screen door that led to the back porch.

By this time, Mom had stepped in front of him on the back porch, blocking him and grabbing his arm to restrain him.

"Please don't embarrass the family, Myron, and please listen," she begged. "Just let it go for the time being. We'll work it out."

He finally relented. "Ok, Mom, I won't do it. But maybe I could just go and talk to him."

"You are not in any condition to talk to anyone right now," Mom suggested.

With reluctance, Uncle Myron yielded to Mom's wishes and averted the family crisis. Uncle Myron did not whip upon Teddy Applegate, I did receive the grades for my sophomore year, and the family name did not become an embarrassment throughout the Vanceburg community.

Uncle Myron would die of a massive heart attack 14 years later in September 1972, at only 47 years of age. Mom would outlive her youngest son by one and one-half years.

Proverbs 29:11: *A fool gives full vent to his anger, but a wise man keeps himself under control.* (NIV)

CHAPTER 18

UNNECESSARILY CONSPICUOUS

Miss Elizabeth Bertram was one of my English teachers at Lewis County High School. I cannot remember the specific year in which I was her student, but it must have been during either my freshmen or sophomore year because, under her tutelage, we studied William Shakespeare. Having taught in at least two public high school situations during my tenure as a language arts teacher, I now know that freshmen study *Romeo and Juliet* and that sophomores study *Julius Caesar*. Miss Bertram was probably in her late 60's or early 70's when I would have had her as an English teacher.

She drove what I recall as being a dark green 1952 or 1953 Chevrolet Bel Air with a power-glide transmission from her residence in Ribolt, near Tollesboro, to Lewis County High School every day. I remember one of her distinguishing characteristics: she wore a very small, quaint black hat with a black bow on the front. Because she always hunched her body over the steering wheel and drove very slowly, never exceeding 30 miles per hour, witnesses to her daily pilgrimage to Lewis Count High School could only see what appeared to be two protruding black ears to the front driver's seat.

Miss Bertram, perhaps because of her advancing age and solitary life as an old maid, did not appear to bathe on a very regular basis and wore very old, outdated dresses that generally fell full-length to the floor, covering entirely her black antiquated pointed toe shoes. She wore very heavy caked on makeup, and generally, perhaps because of her infrequent bathing practices, doused her body with a very cheap but potent perfume that totally permeated the classroom surrounding her. We students made a very conscientious effort to select desks that were between the window and her. When we were on the downwind side, opposite the window side, between her and the door, if a stiff breeze were to sweep throughout the classroom past her and toward the nostrils of the unsuspecting student, the mixture of cheap perfume and pungent body odor was so strong it could almost result in a temporary panic attack.

"Whew! Miss Bertram was ripe today!" students who knew her all too well proclaimed on more than one occasion. This would often spur an ensuing conversation about her personal hygienic practices.

We also had to avoid sitting on the front row in Miss Bertram's class because if she became over excited or animated in her teaching or discipline, she showered the unsuspecting front row victims with miniscule air borne droplets of spittle.

Wayne Reese, her nemesis in the classroom, was always involved in devious or errant behavior; and, I am sure, did his best to make her life as miserable as possible. One memory of him includes the incident that happened the day he smuggled a green snake into the classroom.

Permitted to leave campus during lunch, many of the students would take advantage of this opportunity to visit a small cinder block bar "beer joint" restaurant called the Green Door, diagonally across from the front entrance to Lewis County High School but slightly toward town on Fairlane Drive. Of course, we were not old enough to drink legally, but we could savor the delights of a greasy hamburger and limp French fries, which always seemed more appealing than the lumpy mashed potatoes or clumpy macaroni and cheese offered by the school cafeteria.

On the day in question, Wayne discovered and captured a green snake on his way back from lunch at the Green Door. He calmly placed the object of his attention in his right front trouser pocket and uttered, "I'm gonna' have some fun with this. I am sure Miss Bertram would like to see it," and meandered off to his afternoon class with Miss Bertram.

At the most opportune time, perhaps during her discourse on the Globe Theater or Stratford-on- Avon, Wayne withdrew his prize and released it for the entire classroom to share. Pandemonium erupted in the classroom! Miss Bertram desperately headed for escape toward the door of the classroom; the guys in the class rolled in the aisles, laughing uproariously; and most of the girls jumped up on the chairs, screaming hysterically. The study of Shakespeare was certainly finished for that day.

Another one of Wayne's "moments" brought

excitement and ethical reprimand to everyone in the class when he returned from the Green Door with his collection of Falls City beer cans. He had collected 10 or 12 empty beer cans during lunch and had managed to come early to class on a particular day to deposit the empty beer cans throughout the aisles of Miss Bertram's classroom. When she entered the classroom, she was appalled at the thought that one of her students would be drinking beer.

"Whoever you are, you should be ashamed of yourselves!" she adamantly proclaimed. "Perish the thought that you would be drinking beer at your age and that you would discard your empty cans in the classroom. You are just making yourself unnecessarily conspicuous."

That seemed to be her standard response to every blatant attempt by a student to disrupt her classroom: "You are just making yourself unnecessarily conspicuous."

I also believe, but am not totally sure, that her room may have been the site of the infamous hole in the floor that often served as a source of entertainment for the young ladies who were perhaps fortunate enough to have had an English class in that classroom. It seems that someone had bored a hole through the floorboards, providing clear access to the boy's bathroom directly below her classroom. Often, the young ladies anxiously gathered around the hole to get a glimpse of the urinal below and of any unsuspecting gentleman who may have chosen to use that urinal.

During our year with Miss Bertram, we were fortunate enough to receive exposure to several memorable learning experiences. The first semester, every student had to subscribe to *Reader's Digest*, and we spent most of our time studying to keep abreast of current events, studying the vocabulary exercises, or learning about "The Most Unforgettable Character I Ever Met."

The second semester was much more painful because we had to study Shakespeare. Miss Bertram had visited London, England, including Stratford-On-Avon and the Globe Theater. Of course, she had to tell us about all her visits to the Globe Theater and Shakespeare's birthplace with all the excitement, fervor, and spittle only she could generate.

"Before we begin our study of Shakespeare, I must tell you about my trip to Stratford-On-Avon and the Globe Theater," she would begin.

This generally began a several week study of Stratford-On-Avon because we inevitably kept her going over the same thing for several days. After the first day's lecture, she would begin the second day's activities.

"Yesterday I talked about my trip to Stratford-On-Avon and the Globe Theater," she would begin.

"No, Miss Bertram, you didn't finish yesterday, so you need to continue what you talked about yesterday," we innocently proclaimed. So, she would begin again.

We would stretch out Stratford-On Avon, the Globe Theater, and Shakespeare for several weeks before she finally caught onto our shenanigans. At the end of the year, we would be administered some standard end of the year national standardized test such as the ACT or PSAT over literature and grammar, and nearly the entire class would fail the exam. I am sure she would have been amazed that I became a high school English teacher.

Several years later, burglars invaded her remote residence in Ribolt, KY, and tragically and brutally murdered her. I have often thought about her in the passing years and how so undeserving she was of such a tragic end to her life. She was such a naïve, but gentle, loving, and sweet woman. We just took advantage of her in too many instances.

Titus 2:7-8 explains the characteristics of a good teacher.

> *"In everything set them an example by doing what is good. In your teaching, show integrity, seriousness, and soundness of speech that cannot be condemned, so that those who oppose you may be ashamed because they have nothing bad to say about us."* (NIV)

Wayne Reese, incidentally, became the victim of a very dramatic and tragic automobile accident just a few years after our high school graduation.

CHAPTER 19

THE ROAD NOT TAKEN

I did not immediately enter college after my graduation from Lewis County High School in 1960. At the time, I was working as a disc jockey at the local radio station, WKKS, owned and operated by Karl Kegley. The radio station was adjacent to the swimming pool in south Vanceburg, near what is now the easternmost junction of the Double AA Highway and Fairlane Drive. I had decided to work an extra year at the radio station, not totally convinced I would ever be able to attend college. Though WKKS was primarily a country music station, I was the popular music disc jockey who hosted both a daily evening music show of easy listening music and a top twenty countdown of current pop hits every Saturday afternoon. My job at the radio station provided one added benefit: my numerous fans also frequently enlisted me to serve as the disc jockey for the local sock hops at the Old Mill Building on the riverfront corner of Main Street, opposite the Vanceburg Volunteer Fire Department on Front Street.

I had big dreams of excelling as a popular music disc jockey, perhaps seeing my name in lights and being billed as the next Dick Clark. A major problem was that I did not have a very lucrative salary, since my job at the radio station was only a part-time one. I had no car, which necessitated my walking everywhere: to and from work at the radio station, to and from Vanceburg to my home on Town Branch Hill Road, and to and from any social activity that Vanceburg could provide. To add to the humiliation of being a high school graduate who was still stuck in Vanceburg, when I did have a date, I would have to double date with Larry Denham, Mickey Dunaway, John Gore, or one of my other high school friends who had perhaps returned home from college for the weekend.

My first year after graduation was a miserable experience! I did not have a car, as most of my friends did, and did not have the financial resources to attend college anywhere. I was depressed, stuck in a rut, seemingly with no way out! Perhaps this was why I was so motivated to save as much money as I possibly could.

During that meaningless lost year, however, I made one of the most important life changing decisions I would ever make. Should I take the $600 I had managed to accumulate in my bank account and buy a much needed (and highly desired) automobile, or should I enroll in college, knowing that my $600 account would soon be depleted? Unless you have had to make a similar choice, you cannot possibly fathom how traumatic this decision would be for a naïve 19-year-old Lewis County High School graduate who had to beg for a ride nearly everywhere he went.

Several years later, when I was teaching literature at Lafayette Senior High School in Lexington, the late Robert Frost, in his poem "The Road Not Taken," spoke to the life changing decision I had to make at that time.

> Two roads diverged in a yellow wood,
> And sorry I could not travel both
> And be one traveler, long I stood
> And looked down one as far as I could
> To where it bent in the undergrowth.
>
> Then took the other, as just as fair,
> And having perhaps the better claim
> Because it was grassy and wanted wear,
> Though as for that the passing there
> Had worn them really about the same,
>
> And both that morning equally lay
> In leaves no step had trodden black.
> Oh, I kept the first for another day!
> Yet knowing how way leads on to way
> I doubted if I should ever come back.
>
> I shall be telling this with a sigh
> Somewhere ages and ages hence:
> Two roads diverged in a wood, and I,
> I took the one less traveled by,
> And that has made all the difference.

So, I took my $600 life savings and enrolled as a student at Berea College in the fall of 1961.

Here I am, telling it "ages and ages hence." The road on which I spent my $600 *has made* all the difference.

A quotation from William Shakespeare's *Julius Caesar* *also* speaks to my plight as well. As Cassius, Casca, and the rest of the conspirators are getting ready to engage in and subsequently lose the battle against Marc Antony, Brutus explains to Cassius in Act IV, Scene iii:

There is a tide in the affairs of men,

> Which, taken at the flood, leads on to fortune.
> Omitted, all the voyage of their life
> Is bound in shallows and in miseries.
> On such a sea are we now afloat:
> And we must take the current when it serves,
> Or lose our ventures.

I take pride in the fact, and graciously accept God's providence in the outcome, that I took the tide and current that prevented me from being 'bound in shallows and miseries" for the rest of my life. I thank God repeatedly for leading me to enroll as a student at Berea College.

I intended to pursue becoming a radio announcer and disc jockey, so I would subsequently enroll in every speech, debate, and drama class that Berea College offered.

Berea is a wonderful higher educational institution. I was poor and didn't otherwise have enough money for an education. My only hope for an education was Berea College. I enrolled at Berea with my $600 checking account and graduated four years later with a college diploma and not a penny of college debt: I did not have a single college debt because of the Berea College work-study program. What a ministry to the Appalachian community!

As a bonus, I can wistfully proclaim that today, I proudly posses, not *only* one, but *three* automobiles! In addition, my home is completely debt free. I have truly been a very blessed individual.

Proverbs 8:10-11: *Chose . . . knowledge rather than choice gold, for wisdom is more precious than rubies, and nothing you desire can compare to her.* (NIV)

CHAPTER 20

A FAITHFUL JOURNEY

Romans 11:8-9: *"By faith Abraham, when called to go to a place he would later receive as an inheritance, obeyed and went, even though he did not know where he was going. By faith he made his home in the promised land like a stranger in a foreign country."* (NIV)

By faith, I boarded the Greyhound bus on the Market Street side entrance of Our Kaye's Grill and Bus Station in early August 1961. The restaurant/bus station, strategically located directly across Market Street from Sullivan's Drug Store on the eastern corner, was so named because Kaye was the middle name of Aunt Eula's and Uncle Bill's only "blood daughter," Rhenda Kaye Bonner, who also shared my birth year. Rhenda arrived on the scene on July 31, 1942. I came into being seven days later on August 6. Perhaps, the proximity of our birthdays helps explain why we were always so very close and why she always called me her brother until brain cancer selfishly snatched her from me on January 17, 2013. After all, you must remember that, as I indicated in an earlier chapter, she and

I were "secretly married" by Daddy Ben Flinders when we were mere infants. Our paths were destined to cross each other's from the time of our births until her death.

Melancholy thoughts and feelings of uncertainty, even fear, overwhelmed the meditations of this naïve 19-year-old country boy from Lewis County as the bus departed from the safety and security of Lewis County, Vanceburg, Town Branch Hill Road, and Our Kaye's Grill. This had been my universe for 19 years, the only world I had known, except for an occasional visit to see my dad in Chicago or to visit with Uncle Myron and Marie in Pittsburgh, Pa. Even those visits were "sheltered" because I had always been under the supervision of adults. Now, I was going to be on my own for the first time in my life. The approximate 90-mile trek to Berea would mean bus layovers in what I considered major Greyhound terminals in Lexington and Richmond, so I would spend several hours alone in big bus stations, not the familiar, comfortable one on the corner of Market and Second Street in Vanceburg.

Perhaps Abraham had similar thoughts as he departed the security of Haran to go to a place only God knew. He was acting in faith, going to an unknown new environment, just as I was. I did not know what to expect any more than he did.

In retrospect, I am convinced it was part of God's plan for me to attend Berea College. I would never have been able to complete a college education had it not been for Berea College. It is truly an outstanding educational institution!

The first indication that I was nearing Berea via

old US Highway 25 (This was before I-75 had been constructed.) was the looming water tower that hovered over the southwestern ridge on which both the city of Berea and Berea College were established. Next, there appeared the similarly daunting spire of the main campus classroom building, the *Draper Building*. I would later discover, as I was conducting campus tours during my sophomore year, that the *Draper Building* is a reproduction representation of *Independence Hall* in Philadelphia. Little did I know then that *Danforth Chapel* on the first floor of *Draper Building* would be the very chapel that would witness our wedding vows and launch Donna Tremaine and me on a marital odyssey that would last over 59 years (at this writing). Hindsight, the passage of time, and a changed perspective certainly give a more poignant relevancy to everything, don't they?

The bus approached the gently sloped incline leading into Berea, whizzed past the "Welcome to Berea" placard speedily enough that I barely was able to focus in time to catch its blurred image, slowly reduced its speed to enter campus, and coasted past Blue Ridge Dormitory, Berea College Hospital, and Kentucky Residence Hall. It paused at the first traffic signal, turned left from US 25 onto Scaffold Cane Road, its screeching brakes came to a halt, and its 19-year-old Lewis County wayfarer was deposited on the street corner curb directly across the street from the Carlton Restaurant in Berea, Kentucky. Denny Norris Bonner from Vanceburg, Kentucky, had arrived. He was ready to claim his destiny!

Mom had meticulously packed everything I owned into the shining new, specially purchased 30-inch-long,

15-inch-wide, 12-inch-deep black metal footlocker that had accompanied me on my long arduous journey. My next hurdle was readily apparent.

My conversation with myself began, "This thing is very heavy. How can I pick it up and carry it? I certainly can't lug it very far. Where do I go now? What do I do next? Who do I need to see? How can I get this thing across campus?"

To anyone who had chanced to pass, it would probably have seemed as if I were an alien, deposited in the heart of Times Square in New York City, even though I was merely in Berea, Kentucky, Madison County. I was a wet behind the ear, naïve, nervous country boy from Lewis County. A college with 1,600 students was beyond my realm of comprehension; Berea's student enrollment, in fact, surpassed the 1,526 population of the entire Vanceburg community.

I have since pondered the thought that, if I had arrived in Lexington at the University of Kentucky, with its nearly 30,000-student population, under similar circumstances, my footlocker with my entire personal belongings would have probably disappeared within 15 minutes.

However, you and I both know what happens next! Just when we least expect it, God sends us another one of those everyday ordinary saints to rescue us and take care of us. This time it was a very familiar face, that of my dear cousin Rhenda Kaye Bonner.

While I had spent the last year of my life as a disc jockey at WKKS Radio, contemplating and thinking about the future, she had attended Berea College directly out of high school. She was now a seasoned veteran. My "sister" and "wife" was there to take care of me! I was in safe hands! I was no longer, as Abraham in Genesis, a stranger in a strange land, journeying to a place he did not know. Everything was going to be all right!

Our Lewis County High School graduating class of only 68 students and Berea College would yield the first two members of the Bonner family to graduate from college. Rhenda would graduate in May of 1964 and pursue a 40-year long career as a public health nurse. I would follow a year later in 1965 and become a high school language arts teacher and college freshman composition teacher whose career would also span nearly 40 years.

CHAPTER 21

THE ORGAN FACTORY

All of us have been intrigued and entertained by stories of how other people first met, fell in love, and subsequently spent events in their lives together, perhaps for a very short period or, even less frequently, for half a century or even longer. Thornton Wilder's play *Our Town,* one of my all-time favorite literary masterpieces, superbly addresses this concept through the words of the Stage Manager in "Act Two: Love and Marriage," when he comments on the nature of how significant lifelong experiences are precipitated by tremendously insignificant events. He relates his thoughts to the audience just as George Gibbs and Emily Webb are awakening to a "new day," which just happens to be their own wedding day. The scene subsequently flashes back to recount events that happened on the day when they first "became interested in each other," even though they had lived side by side as neighbors throughout their entire childhood and teenage years. The Stage Manager interrupts a pre-wedding conversation between Mr. and Mrs. Webb:

"Now I have to interrupt again here. You see, we want to know how all this began – this wedding, this plan to spend a lifetime together. I'm awfully interested in how big things like that begin. You know how it is: you're twenty-one or twenty-two and you make some decisions, then whisssh! You're seventy: you've been a lawyer for fifty years, and that white haired lady at your side has eaten over fifty thousand meals with you. How do such things begin?"

I remember how two of my friends, who taught with Donna and me in the college Sunday School Department at Calvary Baptist Church in Lexington, Kentucky, first met. He was a student at the University of Kentucky, and her mother was either a sorority mother or a dorm mother: I do not remember which title was applicable to the circumstances surrounding the actual event. What I do remember, however, is that the young lady, a U. K student herself, was helping her mother host a "social event" somewhere on the U. K campus. Refreshments were being served, and she had volunteered to help her mother serve punch to those who were attending. The young man, on the other hand, was also attending the event, perhaps to scout out all the young ladies who were present to see if any young miss might suit his fancies.

At the most inopportune time (perhaps opportune, depending on how one views the circumstances), just as he was approaching the serving table, she leaned over to dip the serving ladle into the punch bowl to offer him some of its delightful nectar. Her blouse, which apparently was very loose fitting, fell almost entirely to her waist, revealing her upper torso in all its "Maidenform" beauty. Apparently, perhaps because of this experience, he discovered his true love at this very moment. They began dating, fell in love, married, and have now spent most of their lives together. What a wonderful way to meet your future wife! Who would have ever conceived that a wonderful long lasting, Christian marriage would have begun under such a unique and miraculous "Maidenform" experience? Perhaps God does have a sense of humor.

The way in which my wife Donna and I met was not nearly as exciting or unique as this. In fact, it began under very normal insignificant unforeseen circumstances. Donna, at the time, was pursuing the possibility of becoming an organ major during her sophomore year at Berea College, and one of her good friends in the music department was Jeanette Vance. This rendezvous occurred before Donna changed her major to public school music and became a public-school choral music teacher. Jeanette, better known as Gigi, was dating one of my good friends Maw White, who resided, along with the rest of us Aggies, on the first floor of Dana Dormitory, which we simply referred to as Dana I.

We called ourselves Aggies because several of the men on the floor were agriculture majors, and we took tremendous pride in having won and continuing to win the intramural athletic championship for five or six years in a row, before, during, and after our tenure there. We were "supposedly" the ultimate cool guys on campus. At least that is what we thought!

Maw White's actual name was Bill White, but, because he was the expert at making cornbread for all of us Aggies on Dana I, we nicknamed him Maw. In fact, we had an assortment of nicknames for nearly all the boys on the floor. I was Badeye because I could contort my face, and, on command or on a fleeting whim, draw the right eyelid closed, appearing to have a lazy eye. This was my means of either impressing or embarrassing everyone around me, particularly the girls. Robert E. Lee, on the other hand, was "historically labeled," for obvious reasons, "The General." Paul Lewis became Louie, Ronnie Singleton, for reasons unknown by me, became Herm Dog, and his younger brother, Bobby Singleton, appropriately became Herm Pup. Ray Reneau was tagged Taxicab, and Rodney Bussey, the quarterback of our championship tag football team, became Bear. MacArthur Watts answered either to the name of Little Mac or Preacher Mac, which evolved from his role in championing the weekly ritualistic pep rallies that preceded the main athletic event every Saturday. He would elevate us to an athletic frenzy, generally accompanied by the Jaynetts' rendition of "Sally Go 'Round the Roses," played at an unbelievably high decibel level. As you can clearly see, we were quite a consortium of individuals.

Getting back to my story, however, it is important to remember that fellow Aggie, Maw White, was dating Gigi Vance, a musician friend of Donna Tremaine, also known as Trudge, who would later become my wife. Gigi and Donna, as required by the music department of Berea College, were getting ready to attend a music department field trip to a pipe organ factory somewhere in rural Madison County near Berea. Of course, Maw White was to accompany Gigi, but Donna did not have a date, so Maw and Gigi decided that it was an opportune time for Donna Tremaine and Denny Bonner to have a date with each other. My manly ego would like to think that Donna initiated getting us together, but perhaps this is mere wistful thinking on my part.

At any rate, the four of us (Maw, Gigi, Trudge, and Badeye) were to embark on a romantic adventure to an obscure organ factory in a remote rural area of Madison County. I believe, but am not quite sure, that it was located somewhere on Scaffold Cane Road. This certainly seemed to be a very inauspicious event for some very inauspicious characters!

The organ factory was very rustic in nature. It was more like a gigantic warehouse or barn, but it housed all the elements needed to construct a small pipe organ for use perhaps during an Easter morning church service or a rendition of "I'll Fly Away" for a church in some exotic or distant location. I honestly do not remember a great deal about the organ factory.

I do remember, however, that, after the tour, Maw, Gigi, Trudge, and I lolled on the protruding roots of a large sprawling oak tree to enjoy our celestial repast. The food was the normal fare for such an event: cold hotdogs, warm Pepsi Colas, and stale potato chips, along with a "crumbled" chocolate chip cookie.

Nothing about the entire event caused the birds to sing more sweetly or inspired a heavenly angelic choir to lift some heart-wrenching love song toward the passing cumulous clouds that floated across the horizon. I am sure that there was the normal uncertainty and nervousness that accompany the first date, but I honesty do not remember whether Donna and I held hands, walked into the surrounding woodlands, or discovered a private escape where we could savor a stolen moment alone. It was simply a normal spring day spent with normal people doing insignificant normal things. This was my first date with the girl who would later become my wife.

How could I have possibly envisioned that this visit to an insignificant, simple organ factory on Scaffold Cane Road in rural Madison County Kentucky with Maw White, Gigi Vance, and Trudge would become one of the most significant days of my life? It would lead to a lifetime of love, joy, and pain, as well as some momentary intense sadness and disappointment, with my true love, the person God had envisioned for me for my entire life!

The verses from a song, entitled "The Story of My Life," recorded and made popular by Neil Diamond, seem best to describe the impact my wife Donna has had on my life.

> The story of my life
> Is so very plain to read.
> It starts the day you came
> And ends the day you leave.
> You're the story of my life,
> And every word is true.
> Each chapter sings your name:
> Each page begins with you.

Here I am now, over half a century later, and Donna and I have been happily married and intensely involved in the normal daily activities that have cluttered up our lives for nearly sixty years. We have two adult children, both of us have lost both parents to sometimes traumatic and painful deaths, we have both embraced teaching careers that total nearly 80 years of experience in public education, we have experienced both the joys and disappointments of rearing two daughters, and we have together experienced the entire gamut of human experience and human emotions.

Perhaps Proverbs 31:10 would express how God may have envisioned what my wife would really be like many years before we were actually married.

> *"A wife of noble character who can find? She is worth far more than rubies."*

I am sure that I sometimes have an imagination that runs wild, but the lives of my wife and children are so inextricably intertwined with music and theatre that I have humorously envisioned my life as worthy of a Broadway musical. Tracey, a former dance professor and choreographer at Northern Kentucky University, could be my choreographer; Amanda, who is a tremendously gifted singer with music degrees from Shenandoah University in Winchester, Virginia, and Oklahoma City University, could be my featured leading female soloist; and Donna, music teacher and choral director, could be my music director, producer, and director. They would be my production crew. An appropriate title could be *The Story of My Life.* Perhaps, however, *It's A Miraculous Life* would be more appropriate, not because of any miraculous feat on my part, but because God performed many miracles in the life of a once bare foot eastern Kentucky hillbilly, who explored, tamed, and conquered the gently rolling hills of a remote 23-acre farm in Lewis County. God has brought me, as a rural Lewis County tobacco farmer might have proclaimed, "a "pretty fer piece."

CHAPTER 22

SIGNIFICANT LEARNING EXPERIENCES

One of the first students I met at the new student orientation during my first week on campus in August of 1961, certainly influenced my first impression of Berea College. He was a somewhat "rough" handicapped upper classman at Berea when I arrived on campus. I believe he had had polio when he was a child and had to navigate the numerous sidewalks of the Berea College Campus with a very noticeable limp. He was very popular on campus and was always into some kind of mischief. In those days, the college still operated and owned several entities that it no longer operates. One of those was the Berea College Dairy. This young man apparently had an "in" (whether it was legal or legitimate, I have no idea) at the dairy barn, so he provided free milk to all the freshmen boys in Pearson Hall.

During my initial year as a student at Berea, I roomed with my older brother Gary in Pearson Hall on the back of the campus, overlooking the tennis courts, the soccer field, the outdoor track, and the baseball fields. Gary and I were not a good match as roommates and had several arguments concerning what he and I considered a proper time to retire. As a freshman, newly arrived on campus, I did not boast the social network of friends that Gary did, so I was perhaps a little more studious than he was. Often, I would study early in the evening and then go to bed. Gary, on the other hand, would often come in from a date or other social event, turn on the lights, and proceed to study after I had gone to bed. I could not sleep with the lights blaring in my eyes, so we sometimes argued, and I would often leave the room pouting and go sit on the steps that led to the third floor of Pearson Hall until my anger subsided. It seemed, whether true or not, that Gary was completely oblivious to my need for sleep.

The first half of my sophomore year was spent on the ground floor, adjacent to the rear window that exited to the parking lot, of old Howard Hall, a dorm that had been constructed because of a generous gift to Berea College from the Freedmen's Association. Howard Hall was an old outdated white frame structure, demolished very shortly after I graduated to make room for an addition and renovation of the Seabury Building that housed the Athletic Department, the indoor swimming pool, the antiquated Seabury Gymnasium, and the basement locker rooms. The second level of the open Seabury gym gave residence to an ominous circular track that encircled the entire balcony and completely towered over the basketball court on the lower level. This circular track posed a severe problem if a visiting player attempted to take a deep corner shot from the basketball gym proper. The ensuing shot, if it arched too highly, would strike the bottom of the indoor track and, to the chagrin of the unsuspecting opponent, block the shot. Those corners were secret weapons against many a worthy opponent.

In the middle of my sophomore year, I received an invitation to become an Aggie and to reside in Dana Dormitory, one of the newer dorms on campus during my Berea College experience. Dana I became my home for the rest of my college years. It was quite an honor to be a resident of Dana I, which witnessed many outlandish escapades on the part of its residents. One such episode is what I will refer to as the "Dog Food Caper."

Several of the residents of Dana I, many of whom were agriculture majors, also chewed tobacco. It was common practice to be sitting in the TV lounge watching a football game or other athletic event and be "downing" a Pepsi Cola and a bag of Lays potato chips from one of the vending machines. In those days, we would never have thought of having such conveniences as TVs or refrigerators in the room. Instead, we would gather in the basement TV lounge or in someone's room and savor the delights of an occasional box of homemade cookies from somebody's mother or some of Maw White's delicious cornbread. There was even one occasion when someone permanently "borrowed" a pig from the college farm and roasted the entire creature over a gigantic campfire.

One of our fellow Aggies was always very eager to share in these events, especially if food were involved. He seemed to have an almost supernatural instinct for knowing when someone had received a package from home. He would very promptly miraculously appear and make himself readily available to assist in rapidly devouring the contents, often to the chagrin of the recipient. Another fellow student hatched a plan to assist the former in experiencing a significant learning experience.

A long anticipate package from home had arrived, and several of us were sitting around in one student's room enjoying our casual conversation and partaking of the delectable delights when, as expected, our unsuspecting victim entered the room. He had savored the aroma from the far end of the hall and was eagerly anticipating his participation in our celestial repast.

"Did somebody get a package from home?" he asked.

"Yes, I got some homemade cookies," was the response

"Could I have some?" the innocent victim responded

"Sure, you can have whatever you want, but we are having some meat and crackers first. Would you like some of that as well?"

"Yeah!" came the response. "I sure would."

"Here, have a can of potted meat and here are some crackers and a knife."

Innocently received his offering, not even noticing that the label was "mysteriously" missing from the open can, he quickly gulped down the contents.

"Hey, that was really good," He announced.

"Uh, didn't you notice that that particular can did not have a label?" somebody asked.

"Yeah," another interjected. "You just ate an entire can of Alpo dog food!"

"Why do you think there was no label on the can?" someone explained.

"Are you serious?" Our victim gagged, completely deflated.

Conveniently, for him, the bathroom was almost directly across the hall, and he made a hasty retreat. Never again did he rush to someone's room for a snack without being sure of the contents of the "offering" from home.

Proverbs 23:6: *Do not eat the food of a stingy man, do not crave his delicacies; . . . "Eat and Drink," he says to you, but his heart is not with you.* (NIV)

CHAPTER 23

AN EXPERIENCE AT
THE TAB THEATRE

During my last three years at Berea College, my labor assignment was to work in the weatherworn, dilapidated, creaky Tab Theater, somewhat precariously positioned on the backside of the Berea College Campus plateau between two new dormitories, Dana Dormitory on the right and Bingham Dormitory on the left as you faced the theater. I believe, but with some uncertainty, that the Tab had once been an open-air outdoor arena type edifice which had since been enclosed with vertical white sideboard wooden siding that encompassed the rather frail, creaky building. The entire structure was a firetrap waiting to be ignited, and, in fact, did burn to the ground shortly after my graduation.

I had worked as news reporter, disc jockey, and radio announcer at WKKS radio station in Vanceburg during my high school years, so, upon my enrollment at Berea College, my intent was to become a professional radio announcer/disc jockey. I subsequently enrolled in many speech and drama classes. In fact, I may have taken every speech and drama class Berea College offered in its curriculum. This meant that during much of my college experience, I enrolled in drama classes at the Tab Theater. This eventually resulted in my pursuit of a labor assignment at the Tab.

My immediate supervisor at the Tab was Fred Parrot, who taught many of the theatre and drama classes at Berea College and was responsible for either directing or assigning student directors from his classes for all the dramatic offerings of the theatre and drama department. Fred had previously spent one year on a leave of absence in Japan and had studied Kabuki Theater, so some of his theatrical challenges to us as students involved sometimes very experimental techniques and innovative staging challenges. For example, my senior year began with a production of the Greek tragedy *"Antigone."* I do not remember who directed it, but I do recall that the set focused on two gigantic Greek pillars in the center of the stage. The challenge to our directing class was that any subsequent production during that year had to utilize the two pillars as the primary element of its set.

Fred was a truly unique person whose countenance included a rather narrow facial structure with deeply sunken "baggy" eyes and water smoothed brown hair that had begun to show evidence of premature aging around the temples. He combed it straight back from the face and temples, giving the appearance of slightly "bugged" eyes. His face, as I recall, seemed somewhat weathered in appearance. In retrospect, as I reflect on his physical appearance, he reminded me of a slightly aging Richard

Widmark, a movie star, generally a villain, in several 1960's western movies.

Though he was a very astute and knowledgeable drama teacher, when Dr. Parrott lectured or talked for an extended period, saliva would accumulate in the form of chalk colored foam at each corner of his mouth. This necessitated that he always carried with him a handkerchief, and he was frequently required to wipe away the frothy residue.

I admired and respected him a great deal, despite his physical appearance and his antiquated mannerisms; and he apparently reciprocated that respect because he continually cast me in major roles for several of the major theatrical productions, for example, Christopher Fry's *The Lady's Not for Burning* and Shakespeare's *Midsummer Night's Dream*. I even played the title character in Edward Albee's *The American Dream*. I can take pride in the fact that I really *was*, at least at one time, the American Dream. I can boldly recite my favorite line from the show, "I AM the American dream!" and know that it was certainly true.

My directorial skills were on display during my senior year when I chose and directed, as one of the requirements for my class in direction, a scene from Christopher Marlowe's tragedy *Dr. Faustus*, where Satan and his wily assistant devil Mephistopheles tempt and eventually seduce Dr. Faustus by displaying before him the seven deadly sins. Faustus subsequently sells his soul to the devil and suffers the consequences as he is dragged involuntarily off to Hell at the climactic end of the story. My directorial skill resulted in my selection as runner up to the drama department's Hall of Fame director of the year for that particular year. I was "bested" only by a production of a Shakespearean *Fallstaff* adaptation, directed by a faculty member of Berea College. I always felt somewhat cheated because I had had to compete against a faculty member for director of the year.

One of my fondest memories of Fred Parrot recalls an image of him on stage during my technical rehearsal for *Dr. Faustus*. It had been a rather hectic and trying day for him, as there had been continual sporadic crises throughout the day, and he was nearly at the end of his rope. As he was attempting to remedy a problem with the set, perhaps involving the Greek columns, one of the flats fell on him, knocking him sprawling to the floor.

He sprang to his feet, stomping and shouting at the top of his lungs, wiping the frothy foam from the corners of his mouth, and staring google-eyed through the glaring footlights into the vacant auditorium. It is an endearing memory that I still fondly recall.

William Shakespeare: *As You Like It* (Act II, Scene 7, lines 139-143):

> *All the world's a stage, and all the men and women merely players: they have their exits and their entrances; and one man in his time plays many parts...*

Fred Parrot played many roles when he entered and exited my life: teacher, mentor, director, labor supervisor, and good friend.

Proverbs 27:17: *As iron sharpens iron, so one man sharpens another.* (NIV)

CHAPTER 24

THE (NOT SO) INNOCENT SLEEP?

William Shakespeare's words in *Macbeth*, act II, Scene II, lines 49-54:

> *Methought I heard a voice cry, 'Sleep nor more!*
> *Macbeth does murder sleep,'—the innocent sleep,*
> *Sleep that knits up the ravell'd sleeve of care,*
> *The death of each day's life, sore labour's bath,*
> *Balm of hurt minds, great nature's second course,*
> *Chief nourisher in life's feast,--*

In early August 1965, shortly after Donna and I were married, we loaded our entire marital possessions into our two-door lime green 1955 Chevrolet Bel Air hardtop sedan and moved from Kentucky to Lewisburg, Ohio, a few miles west of Dayton. I was employed by the Twin Valley School District in West Alexandria, Ohio, for my first teaching assignment. I became a full-time English teacher who primarily taught sophomore English, but also taught drama and speech, supervised one study hall each day, and directed any plays or drama that I might endeavor to introduce to the patrons of Preble County's Twin Valley North High School. The actual edifice, directly across the driveway from Lewisburg Elementary School, faced Main Street (Ohio Route #503) as it meandered its rather narrow, roller coaster, northerly path between Interstate 70 and Ithaca, Ohio. My actual classroom was located off a very narrow corridor in the extreme left corner of the aging two-story brick structure, adjacent to the study hall.

I still remember Twin Valley North High School as the place where I first experienced the harsh realities associated with my becoming a professional educator. Here, I first stood beside and helped comfort grieving parents who lost their son to a suicide. Seth had been one of my very first drama students and had just completed his leading role in the drama, *The Night of January 16th* when he went home one evening and inflicted a fatal gunshot wound to the right temple.

It was also at Twin Valley North that I was introduced to the psychological damage that could be perpetrated on a very precious, shy, innocent, but beautiful daughter by a morally and ethically depraved parent who "financially coerced" his precious teenage daughter into entertaining men who came to his house seeking a youthful means of sexual gratification. Small wonder that Ellen never wanted to go home.

I experienced a shocking personal confrontation with the reality of the Viet Nam War at Twin Valley North High School. Word filtered back to Lewisburg that Mike Cox, one of my rather promising speech students, had become one of Preble County's first casualties of an impersonal war that raged on an unknown battlefield on the opposite side of the earth, far from the security of his home in Lewisburg.

It was also at Twin Valley North High School that I met my first student nemesis. He was a slightly overweight red-haired, freckle-faced 16-year-old brat who, had he been several pounds lighter, might have resembled a slightly older Opie Taylor from Mayberry, R.F.D. His sole purpose in life appeared to be to inflict torture on me during my first year of teaching. He slept in study hall and in class when I had warned him not to do so and practically dared me to try to awaken him. He talked when told not to, he did not turn in assignments, he always directed inappropriate smart-alecky remarks toward other students, and he always seemed to express himself through some sort of almost heinous sneer. In short, he was totally incorrigible and undisciplined in every way possible and responded negatively to any of my attempts to either appease, console, or direct him through any preferable means.

He even gave me "the finger" through an open school bus window in the presence of some of my other students. He made my life pure chaos, so much so that I even questioned whether I wanted to remain in the teaching profession. I hated him and I hated going to school because of what I knew awaited me. My stomach was always on edge to the extent that I even thought I might have developed an ulcer. I had difficulty sleeping at night and dreaded the sound of the alarm clock that would summon me to my daily routine. I had begun to hate teaching. Even my dreams became susceptible to his intrusions.

"Denny, what are you trying to do?" my wife Donna

screamed hysterically from the pillow beside me. "You are choking me. I could not get you to wake up, and you were choking me. What is wrong with you? Have you lost your mind?"

"What?" I sleepily muttered, fully confused by what she was saying. "What are you talking about?"

"You were strangling me!" she shouted.

"I was strangling you?" I responded in disbelief.

In my retrospective thinking, the episode now reminds me of one of those times all of us have experienced when we have suddenly awakened in a strange motel room or unfamiliar circumstances. We have flailed around looking for the alarm clock or tried to determine the direction of the door or the bathroom? It is as if you are in a totally foreign environment, unable to find your bearings.

I came to my senses and realized that I had clasped my fingers in a death grip around my wife's throat. I *was* choking her. I was determined to vanquish my enemy: my student nightmare.

"I am so sorry, Donna!" I screamed, almost panic stricken. "I was having a terrible dream."

"A dream? What kind of dream would cause you to do something like that?" she prodded.

"I dreamed this horrible student confronted me, and I was strangling him," I responded.

In the ensuing conversation between Donna and me, I learned that I had been desperately choking her for what seemed to her an interminable period before she could awaken me. In horror, she and I realized that I had almost choked her to death because of the emotional trauma inflicted on me by an unruly student.

What would have happened had I been successful in my efforts to strangle him?

I can imagine the cross examination in a court of law. It would probably have gone as follows:

"Now, Mr. Bonner, let me get this straight. You strangled your wife to death because you dreamed you were strangling a student. Is that right?" the prosecuting attorney would ask.

"Yes, sir. I did dream I was strangling him."

"Mr. Bonner, you strangled your wife to death. Do you realize what you have done?"

"Yes, I know what I have done."

"Do you really expect the jury to believe that was the result of an outlandish dream of some sort?"

"It is the truth, sir."

"So, you would have the jury believe you committed murder because of a dream, Mr. Bonner? That will not stand up in court, and you know it."

"I don't know whether the jury will believe that story, sir. But it *is* the truth."

"Oh, come on, Mr. Bonner, you know that is not the truth."

"But it *is* the truth!"

"Well, whether it is or is not the truth, it cannot and will not stand up in a court of law, and you know it."

Yes, I *do know* it now, especially over 50 years later. I can even imagine the lawyers, jury members, and the judge laughing hysterically as I am led away to begin my prison term. Who would really believe I strangled my wife to death because of a dream?

But it was and is the truth! It could have occurred!

My hatred had engendered deep nurtured and dangerous obsessions.

Sometimes our lives reach very precipitous cliffs, and we could innocently embark on very dangerous and different journeys that are emotionally inspired. Where do such dangerous thoughts originate?

The truth is that murder begins in the heart!

Matthew 15:19-20: *For out of the heart come evil thoughts, murder, adultery, sexual immorality, theft, false testimony, slander. These are what make a man unclean;* (NIV)

CHAPTER 25

CLASSROOM WARFARE

Some of my most enlightening and humorous experiences as a teacher occurred when I was teaching Language Arts at Lafayette Senior High School, between 1971 and 1998. During my tenure there, I had several responsibilities other than just teaching Language Arts. My responsibilities included serving as department chairman for most of my time there, approximately 20 years, as well as functioning as student council advisor for about the same length of time. My student council responsibilities at Lafayette eventually resulted in my election as Kentucky Association of Student Councils Executive director for nearly 20 years as well.

I also had the responsibility of monitoring the boy's bathroom directly across from my classroom between classes, a demeaning task that became affectionately known as, and humorously referred to, by those of us who were fortunate enough to have had this awesome experience, "potty patrol." This bathroom, over the years, had become a haven for many of the "secret" smokers, so our principal, Dwight Price, assigned me to do regular checks on the bathroom to ensure that the illegal smokers were discouraged. Now, I must confess that I have had premature gray hair for many years, since my early twenties. In fact, my wife Donna has never known me without some gray shadow in my temples. During my later years at Lafayette, however, my hair color changed to a solid white hue. I discovered, consequently, one day in my bathroom duty, that the derelict smokers had assigned me a new name, a code name warning for the smokers who might be stealing a clandestine nicotine fix in the bathroom. Apparently, the spy appointed to announce my impending arrival had been assigned in advance as I approached the bathroom for one my intermittent inspections.

"Snow White! Snow White!" the appointed sentinel barked out, and miraculously the illicit bathroom activity abruptly terminated.

"And I guess your name is Dopey," I responded, as I entered the bathroom to an abundance of cigarette smoke, but no definite smokers.

Unfortunately, the young man did not understand my obvious reference to one of the seven dwarfs because I received no response whatsoever.

At any rate, I relived the "Snow White" ritual many times during my remaining tenure at Lafayette, whenever I walked across the hall from my classroom to the bathroom.

Preparation for the new school year was a whirlwind of activity. Not only did I have to prepare for my classes, but I also had to attend what seemed interminable meetings: faculty meetings, departmental meetings, student council planning meetings, and in-service meetings. I never seemed to have enough private time for myself at the beginning of the school year, so I often locked my door, turned off the lights, and made it appear that I was not in the room. Eventually, all the business would give way to the first day of classes.

Generally, during the first day of classes, I would deliver a menacing list of anticipated procedures I expected students to follow, many of which would not be acceptable in my class.

"You are not allowed to chew gum," I would announce, beginning my discourse on the evil nature of chewing gum. Then my sarcasm would begin:

"In the first place, chewing gum is a disgusting habit because I have discovered in my years as a teacher that most teenagers do not know how to chew in a mannerly fashion. I know you want fresh smelling breath for that special someone at the locker, but my experience has been that gum chewers are very crude and disrespectful. They tend to blow humongous bubbles and pop them at very inopportune times during class, or they twirl it around their finger, perhaps bouncing it off the desk in the process.

How do you dispose of the gum? I know because I have seen Sally's new white slacks encrusted in gum inadvertently discarded on the seat. Perhaps you discovered that favorite gum stuck permanently to the tread of your Nike sneakers as you hurried across the Lafayette parking lot. Perhaps you have been one of those innocent victims who stored books in the desk only to find Double Bubble or Bazooka stuck to the first 10 pages of his textbook. You see, not only do students not know how to chew gum, but they do not properly dispose of it either. So, if you are ever tempted to chew or pop your favorite gum in class, be prepared for my wrath. When you see me approach you with a piece of scrap paper in my hand, you are to wrap the gum in the paper and deposit it in the trash can."

I had a similar first day discourse for sleeping in class:

"I don't know why, but somewhere in my earlier classroom experiences, I discovered that one cannot learn when one is sleeping in class. Perhaps I had an unhappy childhood experience that warped my mind. Perhaps I am mentally unstable. Perhaps I just have a distorted sense of reality. But somewhere it dawned on me that one could not learn when he was sleeping. What a novel concept!

And why are you here? To learn! Now, some of you will try to outsmart me, but I have become acquainted with your devious techniques in the past. I know that you do not possess x-ray vision that will enable you to read through your hand when it is serving as a visor and covering your eyes while reading during class.

"Furthermore, there are several dead giveaways that you are or have been sleeping. One is the slobbers that accumulates on the desk and indiscreetly flow from the desk to the floor. Others are the student head bob, the accompanying spastic body jerk, and the infamous blood curdling emotional moan that results from a bad dream or sudden awakening.

So, you see, I am at war against sleeping in class. Furthermore, if you do sleep during class, I have devised several weapons to defeat the enemy, sleep. First, I have a spray water bottle that is adequately prepared for the battle. If you do sleep, your dreams may be interrupted by my infamous spray water bottle. You may be rudely awakened by a stream of water cascading down the part in your hair."

Generally, a brief dramatic pause followed, then a challenge to each captivated listener.

"Does anyone in class believe I would not use this bottle?"

At this point, I would holster the spray bottle in my trouser pocket, don my best John Wayne gunfighter pose, and prepare for a display of my "six guns" attack. Only one person challenged me during my entire teaching experience, and that happened to be my own student council president, Ron Smith. I had a wonderful relationship with him, and he thought it would be funny if I drenched him in front of the entire class.

"I don't think you will do it," he proclaimed in the most arrogant voice he could muster.

He got his wish. I drenched him and the entire contents of his desk. The entire class erupted in both laughter and disbelief. They got the message. I'm not sure I ever had to use the water bottle again, but I did have to threaten its use on several occasions. Even Dwight Price, our principal, heard about the infamous bottle and secretly conferred with me.

"Is it true that you have a water bottle and that you threaten students with it?" he asked.

"Yes, sir I do have a water bottle, but I have only used it once that I know of," I responded, explaining its nature and intent.

"You know I cannot support you in this, don't you?" He responded.

"Yes, sir, I realize that." I acknowledged, knowing I was making myself very vulnerable.

I believe Mr. Price understood my madness, but he had carried out his responsibility; he had informed me that I was on my own. That was probably all he wanted.

Another weapon against sleep was an enormous student council gavel that I had commissioned our industrial arts teacher Joe Sparks to make because our student council president was habitually breaking the handle of the small more fragile ones. Flailing the gavel in the air, I would continue my lecture on the dangers of sleeping in class:

> "My second weapon against sleep is this enormous gavel. I have been known to dent desks with this thing. Can you imagine the shock of being awakened by the reverberating sound of this massive weapon as it forcefully assaults the desk on which your head is innocently resting? I would imagine your head would still be reverberating several days later. I am sure you do not want to take that risk. Does anyone not think I would use this?"

Again, I would have to demonstrate the effectiveness of the weapon at hand.

My final weapon for combating sleepiness in my class was fully opening all windows in the classroom to allow cold air to circulate throughout the entire classroom, especially around the sleeping victim. During the winter months, I have witnessed snowflakes falling on an unsuspecting sleeping student's desk as he snoozed away until he suddenly began to freeze.

I would facetiously proclaim to the innocent victim,

"It is difficult to sleep when you are freezing to death and fighting for you very survival, isn't it?"

A submissive nod of the head meant that I had made my point.

Some students, however, learned to plead their case against freezing and selfishly awakened the confused dreamer.

"Oh, no, Mr. Bonner! Please don't open the windows. We'll freeze to death!" was uttered by more than one innocent by-standing student as I menacingly approached the window nearest the perpetrator.

On one occasion, I whispered to the other students, "Please, when the class ends, leave quietly and do not arouse our sleeping beauty. Let's just let him sleep."

He, a senior, awakened about an hour later in the middle of my sophomore English class, wondering and asking, "What time is it? What class is this?"

He had slept through his lunch period and part of another class. What a humiliating experience for a senior to be awakened in the middle of a sophomore class!

My campaigns against sleeping and chewing gum in class were relatively successful. My students learned that I was a formidable opponent.

Proverbs 6:9-10: How *long will you lie there, you sluggard? When will you get up from your sleep? A little sleep, a little slumber, a little folding of the hands to rest —and poverty will come on you like a bandit and scarcity like an armed man.* (NIV)

CHAPTER 26

MENTAL PAUSE

At Lafayette, I became one of the primary teachers of a class labeled Expository Composition, a college preparatory class. It was an excellent class for teaching organization skills, grammar, and syntax, including such essay assignments as extended definition, comparison/contrast, argumentation, and research. One of my most memorable experiences in teaching that class occurred one year during the first meeting of the class.

I had already locked the door, as I generally did, to embarrass late arrivals as much as possible. If someone arrived after class had been in session for a while, the culprit had to knock on the door to gain entry, walk to his seat, and interrupt the entire class. I wanted to make tardiness and promptness an issue. For those who were habitually tardy, I would often lock them out of the classroom for the remainder of the entire class period with an admonition and warning.

> "Since you chose not to be on time
> and to be rude by interrupting the rest

137

of my students, I am going to lock you out of my classroom for the remainder of the class period. You are to sit in this chair outside my room for the rest of the period. If I come out to check on you at any time during the period, and you are gone without my permission, I am going to turn you in for skipping my class. If you need to go the bathroom or request to do anything else, you need to knock on my door and be granted permission. Do you understand that you are not to leave this chair for any reason without my permission?"

Generally, that admonition was enough to ensure that they would be restricted to that seat for the remainder of the class period while they would still be denied access to my class.

"Why are you running to class? Do you have Mr. Bonner?" other teachers often humorously queried my students. They knew my tardy policy.

On the momentous occasion of the previously mentioned memorable experience, I was in the middle of my first day lecture on the evils of chewing gum and the hazards of sleeping in class when a knock on the door came.

"Is this *Suppository Composition*?" a dreadfully late, timid voice asked.

The class erupted in laughter, realizing that "*suppository composition*" was not the same as "*expository composition*."

I am not sure the unsuspecting student even remotely understood what he had said. Such was the nature of language snafus that we often shared in the English Department.

Grace Miller, one my associates in the English Department, shared an experience that happened to her. Apparently, Grace had lambasted a student in class for some disciplinary infraction, and another student had written a note in class to try to calm her friend concerning the purported offense. Grace discovered a sympathetic note left in the desk at the end of class.

"Don't worry about Mrs. Miller's comments. Don't let her get to you. She is probably just going through *mental pause.*"

Perhaps you will agree, as I do, that all of us have gone through moments of mental pause.

Another teacher, my English Department co-chair, shared an embarrassing "tender" moment in her classroom. It seems they were studying poetry at the time, and as is always true when one studies poetry, the conversation inevitably turns to meter and discussions of such scoundrels as blank verse, free verse, and traditional metric forms such as iambic pentameter or anapestic trochaic verse. The challenge is to get students to recognize a metric pattern or verse form and to help them realize that the author did not mistakenly use the vehicle. Sometimes, we teachers resort to personal examples and even to over-exaggeration to get across our message. This fellow teacher was trying to explain how the emphasis on syllables in words would change the entire pronunciation of the word.

"Now, you take a word like *happiness.* The accent on

that word is on the first syllable, causing you to emphasize that syllable more strongly so that it comes out "***hap i ness***." If the accent were changed to the second syllable, it would sound like "ha **pe** nis." (She did not realize, at that moment, that it would sound very much like another word that describes a very private appendage of the male anatomy.). The ensuing snickers and laughter reminded her of her innocent indiscretion.

Other "pearls of wisdom" gleaned from my Lafayette years were that people could "take things for granite," that Lafayette offered a class called *"Music Depreciation,"* and that Shug England, one our English Department teachers, taught *"Moby's Dick,"* by Herman Melville. We were often reminded of the humorous 1965 Bel Kaufman bestselling novel *Up the Down Staircase,* which chronicled the humorous events in the rookie year of the fictional Sylvia Barrett, a teacher at an inner-city school dubbed Calvin Coolidge High in New York City.

Proverbs 25:1: *A word aptly spoken is like apples of gold in settings of silver.* (NIV)

CHAPTER 27

MOVE OVER, RADICAL THINKERS!

As most of you are aware, many extreme radical thinkers have closely scrutinized even modest "Christian overtures" in public education situations over the past several years. These demands have challenged the use of voluntary prayers in many school or public settings, discussions or even a mention of a Christian perspective on "the creation," or even singing Christmas music with any reference to Jesus. A Jewish Rabbi even challenged my wife Donna for allowing her choir to sing "Christian music" during her annual Christmas concerts at Paul Laurence Dunbar High School.

"Are you serious? How can you not sing classical Christmas music during the Christmas season? In fact, we celebrate Christ's birth at Christmas. These are some of the greatest songs ever written. In fact, many of them are established traditions." she responded.

"Well, you need to sing some good Jewish music," challenged the Rabbi.

"Well, you find some good Jewish Christmas music,

and I will sing it," she responded. "In fact, if you were at my concert last year, you would have noticed that we did sing a good Jewish song. I try to incorporate all kinds of music when I can. But there is very little good Jewish ethnic music to select from, and I am not going to compromise the quality of the musical experience of my students by eliminating classical pieces with references to God or Jesus in them," she continued.

She was even questioned one time for her Dunbar choir's rendition of the classic Peter Wilhousky arrangement of "Battle Hymn of the Republic" because the lyrics mentioned the word *Christ* when they said, "in the beauty of the lilies, *Christ* was born across the seas." The critic failed to mention, or at least have enough cultural knowledge to notice, that this passage was part of a very beautiful four-part male voice harmonic section of the anthem.

"My choir will still sing it." she responded. "It is one of the best choral music arrangements of the National Anthem on the market."

The challenge for Christians, or anyone else for that matter, not to mention Jesus, God, or religion when teaching a specifically allusive work of literature, is an even more dubious task. In fact, I often began my introductory remarks to a "challenging" piece of literature with a very carefully worded prologue. Generally, I began with a proclamation of the *Bible* as a literary masterpiece:

> "Let us begin with a little understanding
> of the significance of the *Bible* as a literary
> work of art. First, you must understand

142

that the *Bible* is the all-time best seller; you will find that more copies of the Bible than of any other book. No other book is even close in the number of copies sold. Furthermore, if you were to take out and discard all the theological concepts in the *Bible*, it would still be one of the most significant books ever written. As simply a book of history, it has one of the most accurate and detailed histories ever recorded concerning a single nation: the history of the Hebrew people. It describes with vivid detail the lives of the Hebrew people from the time of the Garden of Eden to the age of the New Testament.

Many critics and scholars also classify the *Bible* as a 'literary masterpiece' containing many literary genres. Many intellectual historians, literary experts, and scholars consider the book of Exodus an *epic*, the Book of Ruth meets all the criteria for consideration as an early *short story*, the Book of Job is generally considered a *poetic drama*, and the Psalms are *poetry*, intended to be sung. In fact, many literary experts classify the Psalm 23, at least in the King James paraphrase, as a nearly perfect poem. There are also several other book of poetry in the *Bible*, including Exodus, Job, Proverbs,

Ecclesiastes, Song of Solomon, and the little book of Lamentations. Furthermore, The *Bible* is also a wonderful book for the study of ethics, philosophy, psychiatry, and morality. You see, even discarding theological concepts in the *Bible* does not detract from its significance as among the most important books ever written. Therefore, it stands to reason that, if you are going to study a masterpiece of literature, you should never exclude the *Bible*."

My students were always amazed and awed about aspects of the *Bible* they had never considered. Then, I could discreetly "home in on" the work of literature at hand.

"Class, today, we are going to begin our study of John Knowles' novel *A Separate Peace*, but first I must explain something else. You see, *A Separate Peace* may have several Biblical allusions, and since I, as a teacher, need to be careful about mentioning religion or the *Bible* in the classroom, I need to explain the word myth. It is *not* a female moth. A myth is a commonly repeated traditional story, which may or may not be true, that attempts to give a simple, easy explanation for a very sophisticated, mysterious, spiritual or intellectual concept. For example, the creation of the world or the Garden of Eden. Since, John Knowles may have made, and probably did make, several Biblical allusions to the Garden of Eden, evil, and the fall of man in *A Separate Peace*, I need to explain to you the Biblical story concerning the Garden of Eden. So, let us, at least for the time being, talk about the Biblical concept of the Garden of Eden. We'll call it a "myth:" a story to explain the complexities of how the human species was created."

Once I gave my introduction, I could then talk about the Garden of Eden with vivid details. I could explain how it was strategically located between the Tigris and Euphrates Rivers, how Adam and Eve lived in peaceful harmony until their temptation by Satan in the form of a serpent, and how their submission to the Devil and temptation destroyed the peace and serenity of the Garden of Eden by introducing sin and death into their world."

After my explanation of the possible "mythological" series of events that ensued in the Garden of Eden, I began.

"Now, let's look at *A Separate Peace*. Does anyone remember where the campus of Devon School, the setting of the story, was in the book?" I challenged.

"Wasn't it located on a river?" a perceptive student responded.

"Actually, there were two rivers. One was the

Naguamsett River and other was the Devon River. Can you Remember? Look on page 68 and find out exactly where the school was located," I further challenged.

"It says Devon School was astride these two rivers," another student answered.

"Yes, that's right! Now, remember where the Garden of Eden was located?" I prodded.

"Wasn't it astride the Tigris and Euphrates Rivers?" came the response.

"Yes. And what was the nature of Adam's and Eve's existence before the temptation by Satan?" I further queried.

"They lived in a perfect society of peace and harmony," another proclaimed.

"And what was the nature of life at Devon before Finny tempted them to jump from the tree, resulting in his own disability?" I asked.

"It was peaceful and harmonious, almost perfect," a student responded.

"What happened after Adam and Eve succumbed to temptation?" I asked.

"Paradise was lost. Submission to temptation destroyed their peace and serenity. Evil and sin, including death, became a part of their lives." another responded.

"And what happened in *A Separate Peace* when Gene yielded to Finny's temptation to jump from the tree into the river?" I further prodded.

"The peace and serenity of Devon were destroyed, and Finny was permanently maimed. Their lives were forever changed," echoed throughout the classroom.

I will not continue the contents of the entire study, but

you can clearly see how the ensuing days would lead to a very perceptive and enlightening educational experience for my students. I never acknowledged or professed directly that I was a Christian in the classroom, but I was able to use the *Bible* and my Christian knowledge on many occasions to shed light on a classic piece of literature such as John Steinbeck's *East of Eden* (See Genesis 4-5) or the anonymous poem "The Destruction of Sennacherib" (II Kings *118-19*).

"You didn't have to verbally tell us in the classroom that you were a Christian," one of my former students would explain several years later, after graduation. "We knew because of how you acted, and what you said. There was never any question about your deep faith," she continued.

Radical thinkers or no radical thinkers, there were ways in which I was able to discreetly, legally, and academically make my faith abundantly apparent to my students and enhance their educational experience as well. I then was able to expand their minds and assist them in pursuing new avenues of intellectual exploration. That is what "real" education encourages!

CHAPTER 28

A NEW DIMENSION OF TEACHING

When Lafayette Principal Dwight Price first approached me about becoming Lafayette Student Council advisor, I could never have imagined that this would enable me to become a much better teacher. This opportunity opened a completely new dimension of teaching that, I believe, enriched my spiritual, psychological, and emotional growth. I had always been a taskmaster of a much-focused atmosphere in the classroom. I was a no-nonsense, very demanding and disciplined teacher whose focus was only on the academic, intellectual, and scholarly aspects of teaching. Sometimes, this atmosphere, even though I tried to establish an amenable and friendly relationship with my students, did not permit me to have a very good understanding of the private lives of my students or a very intimate relationship with them as individuals. This all changed dramatically when I became a student council advisor. I began to know my student council members as warm social beings and not just academic machines.

One of the lessons that both my student council

members and I had to learn was the dual expectations that sometimes accompany being a teacher. I needed to be demanding in the classroom, but more casual outside the classroom in less formal settings such as state conventions, national conferences, or banquets. I explained my expectations in the classroom this way:

> "Please understand that as a teacher, I must maintain a certain distance from you as students in the classroom. I cannot demand respect and order in the classroom and be your best pal at the same time. I cannot get "too close" to you in the classroom in the presence of other students. It is somewhat like what I refer to as aesthetic distance in the theater. If you sit on the front row of the theater, you see all the grease paint, eye shadow, and facial make-up; and you might be the unexpected recipient of spittle mist when the soloist sings "Master of the House" from Victor Hugo's *Les Miserables*. In addition, you will suffer tremendous neck and shoulder discomfort from having to strain to look up to the stage. On the other hand, if you sit on the very back row of the theater, you often cannot see the minute facial expressions of the actors, nor can you hear many of the subtleties of the spoken dialogue. You often cannot hear very well at all.

Consequently, the best seat in the house, for me, anyway, is the one in the middle section of the theater about halfway back. This is what I call aesthetic distance. This is what my role must be as a teacher. I need not be too close to you as students, but at the same time, I need not to be too far away either. In the classroom, you will be expected to call me Mr. Bonner, but you may call me by my first name at conferences, conventions or other outside social functions, especially when students from other schools call me by my first name, as they often do."

On multiple occasions, I have encountered students outside the classroom in social settings, very different from those in the classroom, where students recognized me as a "real" normal human being.

"Mr. Bonner, I saw you at Fayette Mall last Saturday at the food court!" exclaimed one of my students.

"Yes, my wife lets me out of the house on special occasions, and I am allowed to be a normal person. I even go shopping for groceries at Kroger sometimes," I responded.

"Oh, Mr. Bonner, that is not what I meant, "she countered.

"I know. I am just teasing," I acknowledged. "I was just trying to make the point that we teachers are normal. We have private lives like everyone else."

Generally, my students knew when, where, and how

to address me. Even when other students from across the state, whom I knew on a more casual basis, called me "Denny," some of my students, even then, could not foster the courage to address me in that manner. Sometimes, even today, in a mall or restaurant, I will casually meet a former student, who may now be forty or fifty years old, but cannot address me in any way except as "Mr. Bonner."

In November 1979, at the annual state student council convention, advisors from across the commonwealth of Kentucky, elected me to become Executive Director of the Kentucky Association of Student Councils, a conglomerate collection of members from private and public schools ranging in location from Ashland to Paducah. For the next nineteen years, until my retirement from Lafayette in 1998, I served the state in this capacity. This meant that I was responsible for planning a Kentucky Association of Student Councils summer leadership workshop each year, serving as the official in charge of the Kentucky delegation to the National Association of Student National Conference each summer, and organizing and planning the annual Kentucky state convention each November. In this capacity, I had the opportunity to personally meet and enroll in leadership seminars under the tutelage of such notable people as then United States President Ronald Regan, UCLA legendary basketball coach John Wooden, or first female U. S. Supreme Court Justice Sandra Day O'Conner. In my advisor capacity, I was privy to attend a seminar with noted philosopher and teacher Leo Buscaglia, author of "Living, Loving, and Learning" and "The Fall of Freddy the Leaf," a parable about death and its acceptance.

These people significantly and positively affected my life and assisted me in becoming a better teacher and better human being. It became my custom, when someone made a significant contribution to my life or touched my life in a meaningful way, to give them a Golden Rule Marble, which simply displayed "Do unto others as you would have them do unto you" inscribed on its exterior band. I always challenged them with the expectation that, when someone touched them in a similar manner, they, in turn, should bestow the Golden Rule Marble to that person. They were not supposed to keep it but were to pass it on. I would like to think I still have Golden Rule Marbles in circulation throughout the United States, touching other people's lives, even after all these years. One of the life-altering spiritual rewards of student council work was that I learned to appreciate more fully the humanity of other people, particularly my students.

In the spring student council election of 1990, Lafayette elected an all-female slate of executive officers for the 1990-91 school years. These eager young ladies assisted me in changing the nature of student council at Lafayette dramatically. In several prior years, I tried unsuccessfully to implement a student council retreat to kick off the school year. I explained that we could use this time for goal setting, planning all our student council calendar activities for the entire year, and orienting and training both the new officers and the newly elected regular student council members. We could use the event to motivate them with increased energy for the coming year, encourage them to enjoy each other and have fun, and promote bonding the group into a close "family unit," prepared to face the joys and challenges of a new school year. I was serving as Executive Director of the Kentucky Association of Students Councils at the time. I first conceived the idea when I attended one to the leadership training sessions at the National Conference, held annually during the last week of June.

That year, in the summer of 1990, some of the student council girls returned from the National Association of Student Council National Conference with a new determination to host a fall retreat. The chairperson of the retreat committee, and I, along with the other officers, enthusiastically endorsed the idea and began consummating plans for the first of many ensuing student council fall retreats. We secured all the needed parental permission slips and received approval from the Fayette County Board of Education for our one/half day absence from classes in early September. We obtained all the food and planning materials needed for the nearly two-day event, including enough food, supplies, tents and sleeping bags, to serve as lodging for all delegates, and arranged for school bus transportation for all 75 student council members to Natural Bridge State Park, near Slade, Kentucky. On the designated Friday afternoon in the fall of 1990, we eagerly welcomed the yellow school buses that were to transport us on our odyssey to the campground of Natural Bridge State Park.

Upon arrival, we set up our "tent city" in a small clearing amid the fading shadows of a cluster of oak trees adjacent to the bathhouse that would provide restroom amenities and freshly showered bodies after our steamy planning sessions in the September afternoon heat. We attended goal setting sessions, officer-training sessions, calendar planning seminars, and of course, participated in our own "Crazy Olympic Games," complete with improvised banners and group cheers. We even had a session that would help us to cooperate more effectively with the Lafayette faculty and administration. One afternoon was set aside for two hours of recreational time so that students could meander along one of the many hiking trails or perhaps scale the mountain to enjoy a panoramic view of the trees and valley from atop Natural Bridge itself. Our final night included a bonfire session with all of us sitting or standing around the campfire, reflecting on the events of the entire weekend experience and thanking those who had influenced our lives during the festival of activities.

"Mr. Bonner, would it be alright if we stood around the campfire, held hands and prayed?" one officer asked. She knew that I was a Christian, as did all the other students in attendance, but was also sensitive to the fact that I could not place myself in the uncomfortable situation, as a public-school teacher, of planning and leading a Christian activity.

"Sure, I have no problem at all with it. You realize I cannot plan or lead it. You will have to lead it yourself or have someone else lead it spontaneously, and you cannot force anybody who does not want to participate to do so. It must be strictly voluntary, and we cannot make anybody feel uncomfortable. I can participate, but I cannot lead it because of the "supervised religion issues" within the public-school venue. I know you understand." I explained.

"Yes." she responded. "You won't have to lead it. I'll lead it."

Thus began one of most meaningful annual traditions that emerged from our first student council retreat. I will never forget the "spiritual high" I received from witnessing 75 high school students who clasped their hands together around a campfire and lovingly prayed for themselves and each other as the campfire faded to dying embers, and the twilight shadows began to settle into the oak infested forest and invade our camp. I do not recall that a single student failed to participate. It was a truly beautiful experience.

Remember what Jesus said about prayer?

Matthew 18:20: *Where two or three come together in my name, there am I with them.* (NIV)

I believe God was with us in those intimate moments and hopefully in the lives of many family's members who themselves were not really with us. I did not have to lead: they resolved the situation.

So, you see, some of my most meaningful and fulfilling experiences as a teacher did not evolve from any extended study of Shakespeare's *Julius Caesar*, instruction in the use of proper organizational skills in *Expository Composition*, or in those "Ah, ha!" moments that sometimes resulted from an original thought in my Logical and Critical Thinking class. Those moments were always gratifying in a very special way, to be sure. Through my personal, often spiritual, connections with my students, however, I became a better teacher and person. My students affected and helped me just as much as I affected and helped them.

CHAPTER 29

FEBRUARY 21, 1973

Genesis 1:27: *So, God created man in his own image, in the image of God created he him; male and female created he them.* (KJV)

Genesis 2:7: *And the Lord God formed man of the dust of the ground, and breathed into his nostrils the breath of life; and man became a living soul.* (KJV)

In 1972, after Donna and I had been married for 7 years and after we had tried unsuccessfully several times to have children, our family doctor told us that we would never be able to have any children of our own. He reluctantly informed us that my sperm count was too low for Donna to conceive and that it might be more advisable for us to consider adoption as a means of fulfilling our desire to have a family. At that time, we were members of Gardenside Baptist Church in Lexington, and I was seriously praying about the possibility of my being ordained and serving as a deacon at Gardenside Baptist. I had prayed several times, asking God to give me a sign of what I should do.

I had asked several times for God to give me some trivial sign of some sort, and each time God confirmed my request. However, nothing that I asked for was of any miraculous nature at all, so I explained away the results as simply coincidental. Finally, I propositioned God. (By the way, I would not encourage you to proposition God, partially because I really do not believe in bargaining with God and partially because He might accept the terms of your bargaining and grant what you have requested. You certainly need to be cognizant of the fact that He *can do* what you have asked.) At any, rate I propositioned God. I could not believe what I was doing. If He wished me to become a deacon, I needed Him to do something entirely beyond any logical or human explanation. Therefore, in a moment of disbelief and, in expectancy, I discussed the situation with God, reasoning that, if He would allow Donna to conceive a child, I would certainly take this as "miracle enough:" proof that He wanted me to serve as deacon.

Would you believe that Donna discovered in the next several days that she had in fact conceived? Moreover, miracle of miracles, I made the bargain, and the events unfolded without Donna's knowledge. I did not even tell her about the events until after the doctor had revealed that she was expecting. She was in shock when I explained the entire arrangement with her. I even agreed to become a deacon at Gardenside Baptist Church. Our miracle, however, was not even close in nature to the "miraculous conception" of Joseph and Mary when Jesus, the Son of God, was born to them. I do believe, nevertheless, that Donna's conception was a miracle. God was and still is in the business of performing miracles.

Around 8:00 on February 21, 1973, as Donna's labor pains were reaching their apex, she and I frantically navigated the rapidly closing railroad barriers on Waller Avenue in our frenzied odyssey to the Central Baptist Hospital Maternity Ward. Our 1965 navy blue Chevrolet Malibu surely was a model of efficiency and expediency as we twisted and turned to maneuver our way around the closing railroad gates and the distantly approaching freight train.

Tracey Leigh Bonner promptly informed the world of her arrival an hour later at 9:03 p.m.

Shortly after Tracey's birth, a friend and fellow choir member from Gardenside Baptist Church called Central Baptist Hospital to find out whether Donna Bonner had delivered her baby. The receptionist gave Donna's room number and revealed to her that Donna had given birth to a baby boy. The next day, to Donna's chagrin, our friends and acquaintances bombarded the hospital with gifts celebrating Tracey's arrival. The problem was that all the gifts were blue in nature. I learned for the first time that baby girls should receive pink, yellow, or pastel-colored gifts, certainly not blue ones. Blue is a boy color. However, we soon solved the dilemma when we discovered that two Donnas shared the same room: Donna Bonner had given birth to a baby girl, and Donna Kotar had delivered a boy.

If you are an avid University of Kentucky football fan, as I am, you will surely recognize the name Kotar because Doug Kotar, Donna Kotar's husband, was a running back and return specialist on the University of Kentucky football team. He is in the record book at UK because the first time he received a kickoff, he promptly returned it 98 yards for a touchdown against the Clemson Tigers. He had an outstanding college career at UK and went on to play several years of outstanding professional football for the New York Giants. Tragically, he died while undergoing physical therapy and chemotherapy for an inoperable brain tumor in 1983.

On this February day in 1973, however, the name Donna Bonner did not enthusiastically appreciate being mistaken for Donna Kotar. The name could have been Donna Reed or Donna Summer, and the result would have been the same.

I believe I was more aware of the reality of God's sovereignty and power at Tracey's birth, than at any other moment of my life. I marveled at the tiny fingers and toes, the perfectly formed arms and legs: this tiny, fragile, wrinkled miniature human being. I remember driving home alone from the maternity ward with just God and me in the car, and, as I passed Turfland Mall on Lane Allen Road, joy and amazement overwhelmed me, tears of joy and thankfulness streamed down my cheeks rendering Lane Allen Road nothing but a blur.

"Only God could perform such a miracle as childbirth." I uttered to myself.

Only God could later transform such a vulnerable, dependent tiny creature into a fully developed human being. Tracey, as a child would dress up in her mom's high heeled shoes, she would almost total her 1974 yellow WV Beetle, attend the Lafayette Junior-Senior prom with two dates, and drive off to college by herself, for the first time, to Shenandoah University in Winchester, Virginia.

She would grow up to live, not only in Winchester, Virginia, but also in New York City; Irvine, California; Grand Junction, Colorado; Memphis, Tennessee; and Wilder, KY.

Science enables human beings to develop cures for debilitating diseases and engineer vehicles that can soar to 30,000 feet or even to the moon. We can even create artificial limbs and organs that can almost rival real ones and utilize technology to build almost insurmountable skyscrapers such as the Sears Tower in Chicago, the Empire State Building in New York City, or even the World Trade Center Buildings in New York City. However, something is even more amazing! Only God has been able to create life! Only God can create a living soul. Only God can make a living, breathing, flesh and blood human being. Only God can arrange for the development of a fragile miniature human being into a fully adult one. Only God can provide victory over death and bestow upon us life eternal.

CHAPTER 30

CINDERELLA

It was a very warm spring like day, either in early December or in early April. I do not remember the specific day or year, just that Tracey was probably around 4 to 6 years old at the time. That would place the sequence of events as having occurred sometime between the fall of 1978 and the spring of 1981. I do distinctly remember, however, that I had decided to take advantage of the pleasant weather and give a good cleaning to our navy blue 1964 Chevrolet Malibu. Perhaps I desired to wash away the early December road grime or the winter's accumulation of road salt.

You need to know when I wash and clean a car, I really wash and clean! I begin the process by cleaning the insides of all the windows, polishing all the vinyl/leather interior features, vacuuming the interior carpeting, cleaning the brake dust from the wheels, and washing and waxing the unsuspecting vehicle. I even clean and vacuum the trunk. My older daughter Tracey now refers to my very thorough cleaning process as "the Denny

Bonner treatment." In fact, both of my daughters claim, even to this day, that nobody can clean a car as thoroughly or make it look any better than I can. In moments of weakness, I have yielded to requests from my daughters and given "the Denny Bonner treatment" to vehicles in several locales, including Winchester, Va., Laguna Beach, Ca., Oklahoma City, and condominium parking lots in Grand Junction, Colorado, and Memphis, Tennessee. I need to pinpoint on a USA map all the locations where I have cleaned vehicles for my daughters.

On this day, I garnered all the needed cleaning supplies and embarked on my quest to restore, as best I could, the original beauty and luster of the Malibu. At some point in the washing process, Donna and Tracey exited the garage door with the proclamation than Tracey was going to assist me in washing the car.

"Tracey wants to help you wash the car," Donna announced. "I am cleaning the kitchen, and she is getting bored, so maybe the fresh air and playing outside will be good for her."

"Sure, no problem," I agreed, knowing that his probably meant trouble because Tracey could not resist the opportunity to wield the water hose, and inevitably the two of us would end up with a thorough soaking. Nevertheless, I agreed, and we proceeded together to wash the car: bonding time for the two of us.

"Tracey, I'll wash the front fender of the car, and then you can rinse off the soap."

We agreed to this arrangement, until we could eventually complete the task at hand, washing off the grime and dirt to my satisfaction. I proceed to soap down each section, and Tracey followed behind in her Cinderella outfit rinsing each one and dousing both of us in the process. We ultimately retired the hose, and I began the drying process.

"Dad, can I walk down to the corner and back?" Tracey queried.

"Sure," I responded. "Just do not go into the street and turn around at the corner and come straight back."

"I will," Tracey innocently announced, and she headed off to the corner of Maywick Drive and Appomattox Drive, five houses down from my driveway.

"Do not cross the street and be very careful," I cautioned, knowing that she would be in my range of vision the entire time.

"OK!" she replied and excitedly meandered down the driveway toward the sidewalk, fully adorned in her frilly pink Cinderella outfit that had adequately served as her queenly attire the previous Halloween. I continued drying the car to my satisfaction and perfection, preoccupied with the task and very oblivious to the passage of time or to Tracey's whereabouts.

Several minutes later, Donna emerged from the house.

"Where is Tracey?" she asked.

I was suddenly jarred back to reality by the fact that I had forgotten about Tracey and that several minutes had passed.

"She decided to walk down to the corner," I explained. "She should be back any minute."

I tried in vain to console myself and, simultaneously, to assure Donna that I had not been negligent in my indiscretion.

"You let her walk down to the corner by herself?" Donna sternly admonished.

"It is only five houses," I explained. "She should be alright. I told her not to cross the street and to come straight back."

Donna walked to the end of the driveway and glanced down the street toward the corner.

"Denny, I don't see her anywhere." Donna nervously explained.

I desperately joined her at the end of the driveway, and, to our mutual dismay, Tracey was nowhere! We glanced down the street in the opposite direction. No Tracey!

"I'll walk down to the corner and see if I see her on Appomattox Road," Donna responded.

I, meanwhile, walked in the opposite direction toward Beacon Hill Road to see if she had perhaps returned and gone in that direction.

A few minutes later, we met back at the entrance to the driveway, but neither of us had seen any trace of Tracey. I had also checked all the side streets between our house and Beacon Hill Road, and Donna had turned the corner at Appomattox and walked up to the corner of Alexandria Drive, one of the most highly trafficked streets in our neighborhood, but she saw nothing of Tracey.

Now we were in a state of panic! All kinds of desperate thoughts crept into our reality. Could she have crossed the street and walked toward the Kroger grocery store less than a quarter of a mile away? Could she have turned right at the corner and walked toward Fredericksburg Road? Even worse, could some stranger, perhaps a child predator or pedophile, have picked her up in his car? We imagined the worst.

"I am going to walk to the corner and walk up to Alexandria Drive!" Donna practically shouted.

Simultaneously, I jumped in the car, desperately turned the ignition key, started the engine, jerked the car into reverse, and backed from the driveway. Then I sped hysterically down Maywick Drive toward Beacon Hill Road. Reaching the end of Maywick Drive, I turned right on Beacon Hill toward Lane Allan Road, then right on Lane Allan, and began to circle of the block.

If I did not see her, I reasoned, I would retrace my trail and circle the block in the other direction. Surely, she would be either on one of those two blocks or on one of the side streets. After all, she had been gone only a few minutes.

My heart was beating frantically, and I felt the warmth of the tears that had begun to flow down my cheeks. "Why did I not pay closer attention to where she was? Had I failed the ultimate test of being a good parent? How could I have been so irresponsible?" I began to reprimand myself psychologically as visions of her abuse at the hand of a total stranger encompassed me.

Suddenly, through my blurred vision, I became vaguely aware of a tiny, miniature creature approaching from the opposite direction. Then, the Cinderella clad toddler came into clear focus. I recognized the Cinderella attire! Tracey had decided to circle the entire block. She knew exactly where she was and what she was doing. She was not lost. She was safe. Her desperate father had found her. Tears of joy flooded my face, and Tracey received what, I believe, is the one and only whipping I ever administered to her.

The words, "This hurts you more than Me." certainly rang true. It really did hurt me more than it did her. I was just glad to see her safe and alive. It is very difficult to spank a child when you are only happy that you have found her.

Proverbs 23:13-14: *Do not withhold discipline from a child: if you punish him with a rod, he will not die. Punish him with a rod and save his soul from death.* (NIV)

CHAPTER 31

HE (SHE) NEVER FAILED ME YET!

My younger daughter, Amanda Jennings Bonner, born on January 11, 1980, entered the world with somewhat of a handicap because she received my grandmother's first name Amanda and my mother-in law's maiden last name of Jennings. Nobody could, or should have been, expected to live up to the expectations that are associated with those two names!

At first, Amanda was the eighth wonder of the world for Tracey, seven years her senior. Tracey was simply fascinated to have a baby sister who could serve as a real live Barbie Doll. Tracey would hold Amanda for seemingly endless periods, at least until Amanda began to cry. Then, Tracey would promptly discard her baby sister in favor of something much quieter and more docile. In fact, Tracey would later claim credit for Amanda's vocal prowess at beautifully rendering a soprano solo aria or Negro spiritual because Tracey mastered the art of knowing how to make Amanda scream and wail at the top of her lungs.

"She would not be able to sing the way she does if it

had not been for me," Tracey would later brag. "I helped to develop her lungs and her singing voice by knowing exactly how and when to pester her until she screamed at the top of her lungs. She would not have the beautiful solo voice she has had it not been for me."

Amanda did develop into quite a gifted soloist. Who could have ever conceived, at these early Tracey training sessions, that Amanda would sing the national anthem for an Elizabeth Dole campaign swing through Lexington on behalf of her husband, U. S Presidential candidate Bob Dole, or that she would garner the lead role in the musical production of *Anything Goes* at Dunbar Senior High School in Lexington?

John Akers, the former head principal at Dunbar, reminds me nearly every time I see him of how Amanda developed a severe nosebleed when he attended the Dunbar production of *Fiddler on the Roof.* She just kept singing without any hesitancy at all. She just wiped the blood from her nose and kept on singing.

His opening question always is, "How is Amanda?

"She is doing well. In fact, she is in her second year at Shenandoah University and Conservatory in Winchester, Virginia, and is still singing in musicals. She is probably going to major either in Musical Theater or Vocal Performance." I responded.

"I will never forget the time she developed a nosebleed in the middle of the show and just kept right on singing," he remembers. Then we lapse into a conversation about Amanda's future: perhaps where she will next perform.

I have always been very proud of all of Amanda's musical endeavors in the music department of Paul

Laurence Dunbar High School, but I believe one of my proudest moments was when she sang the solo for the spiritual "He Never Failed Me Yet" from noted composer Robert Ray's *A Choral Tapestry*. Donna was serving one of several stints as interim minister of music at Calvary Baptist Church in Lexington and was leading the sanctuary choir at Calvary at the time.

Since Amanda was one of the best soprano soloists in chorus at Dunbar High School, Donna, acutely aware of Amanda's vocal gift as a soloist, called on Amanda to accompany the Calvary Baptist Sanctuary Choir as featured soloist. Amanda knocked it out of the ballpark. Normally the congregation of Calvary Baptist did not respond with applause, but this anthem and solo resulted in a thunderous ovation from the entire congregation. It was a truly worshipful experience. In addition, the church service aired on WVLK Radio in Lexington to the entire Metro-City area. I could not have been prouder!

Psalm 95: 1-3: Come, let us sing before the Lord; let us shout aloud to the Rock of our salvation. Let us come before him with thanksgiving and extol him with music and song. For the Lord is the great God, the great King above all kings. (NIV)

CHAPTER 32

A CAUTION SIGN

James 4:13-14: *Now listen, you who say, 'Today or tomorrow we will go to this or that city, spend a year there, carry on business and make money.' Why you do not even know what will happen tomorrow. What is your life? You are a mist that appears for a little while and then vanishes.* (NIV)

Even though I recently reduced the strenuous nature of my physical workouts because of a stress fracture on the second toe on my left foot, for the last 40 years or so I have been an avid jogger and runner. Currently, during the winter months, my regimen includes a 1 mile, 16-minute workout on the elliptical machine at the YMCA in Beaumont Center, with a 1 mile rather fast paced walk on the treadmill nearly every day, and a 2-mile trek on the bicycle machine. In addition, I have a regimen of several minutes of extensive warm-up exercises that either precede or follow the actual workouts. Sometimes, in the past, I became a little erratic in my physical activities in the fall and winter months when the weather did not cooperate, though I never totally abandoned them. In fact, Donna and I both joined the Silver Sneakers Program of the YMCA, which provided free membership to the YMCA through our health provider United Health Care. Now I do not miss many days of some form of physical exercise.

In the fall and summer of 2004, I was jogging at least 3 miles and walking 1.5 miles per day, and my heart rate/pulse normally averaged between 45 and 50 beats per minute. I thought I was in very good physical condition and naively had never questioned my immortality.

The fall semester for the Fayette Public Schools began as usual around the middle of August in 2004. I had already retired from teaching language arts at Lafayette Senior High School and was then teaching freshmen composition at Eastern Kentucky University in Richmond, KY, making the approximate 90-minute round trip commute to Richmond every Tuesday and Thursday. In addition, as usual, my wife Donna recruited me to help rearrange some of the classroom furniture, bookcases, books, and pictures for the new school year. One of my responsibilities was to rehang all the pictures in her choral music room at Paul Laurence Dunbar High School. Each year, she had a new picture made of both that year's chorus and choir, and the new pictures necessitated rearranging and rehanging almost all the pictures each fall. I would borrow the tall stepladder from the gym, climb to its upper extremities, stretch as much as I possibly could, drill new holes in the grey cinder block walls, and rearrange the entire display of approximately 25 to 30 large framed and heavy pictures.

In September 2004, I strained myself in stretching to hang one of the large, cumbersome pictures and apparently overextended a muscle in my left chest, pulling it, resulting in minor pain for several weeks. The pain was not very severe, and I waited for the irritation to subside while I continued my regimen of jogging and exercising each day. About 2 weeks later, Donna became worried about my slow recuperation and recovery.

"Maybe, you should schedule an appointment with the doctor," she suggested

"No, I don't think I need to do that. It will go away eventually after it has had time to heal," I reasoned. Remember, most men always put off going to the doctor as long as possible!

Two weeks later, however, the discomfort was still there. I could not really describe it as pain, but it was more of a discomfort or irritating menace that just did not seem to give any indication of going away. I called our family physician and explained everything to him. He scheduled an appointment and called me into his office.

During the ensuing physical exam, he questioned me extensively.

"What does it feel like?" he asked

"Well, to me it feels like a strained muscle," I explained.

"Is it a severe pain?" he further queried.

"No. It is just a source of irritation," I responded.

After the perusal examination, his response verified what I thought. "I don't see any apparent muscle strain or damage. What about your family history?"

"Well, my father passed away of a heart attack at age 54, and my mother also died of a heart attack at age 74," I explained.

"Maybe we should do an EKG," he suggested. "Your health, for your age, is very good; and you are in very good physical condition, but you have never had an EKG," he stated. "With your family background and your age, that might be a good idea, even though I really don't expect to discover any problem." He did an EKG on the spot.

"There is something that looks a little suspicious here," he told me. "Let's schedule you for an additional, more accurate test."

He scheduled me for a myoview heart stress test in two weeks and assured me he would be there during the entire procedure, which would require a 4-hour block of time. I could not eat anything for several hours prior to the actual test.

I reported to the Lexington Clinic East two weeks later for the procedure. The test stipulated that my heart rate had to reach a certain rate (I believe it was 130 heartbeats per minute) on a treadmill. Once the heart was beating at the elevated rate they desired, they would inject a radioactive substance, I would exercise for another short period, and then go into another examination room where they would take a series of pictures of the heart. Following that series of pictures, I would rest until the pulse rate subsided, and then they would take another series of pictures of the heart at rest. Once the task was completed and the results compiled, the doctor would inform me of the results once he had had an opportunity to discuss them with a cardiologist. The next day, I received the phone call from my family doctor.

"The myoview test shows what may be some blockage to one of your arteries. We are not entirely sure of what is there, if anything, but we have scheduled you for a heart catheterization with the cardiologist to make sure," he informed me.

"There must be some mistake!" I exclaimed to Donna. "Perhaps they looked at the wrong chart. Maybe they confused my chart with someone else's. I have never had any evidence of any heart problems. I am in excellent physical condition. In fact, I am running and walking over 4 miles per day. How can this be possible?"

On October 13, 2004, Donna and I reported to the cardiac ward of St. Joseph Hospital in Lexington for my heart cath. Of course, my "other wife" Rhenda was there for me, as she always has been.

"I want you to be sure of one thing about this procedure," the cardiologist began. "When we do a procedure of this sort, if we find anything wrong, we will correct it on the spot. You will be unconscious so we will not be able to get your approval. We will just go ahead and do what we need to do. So, you need to sign this statement allowing us to do whatever we need to do," he explained

I signed the statement in front of Rhenda and Donna, fully expecting that the doctors would find nothing wrong. The anesthetist injected the numbing ingredient, and I soon drifted into unconsciousness.

I awakened several minutes later as the proud (perhaps not so proud), recipient of a heart stent in one of my major arteries. It had had a 90% blockage! I had been running and jogging 4 miles per day and could have suffered a major heart attack at any moment. I was in total shock. I had flirted with death and won!

The doctor showed me the photographs to substantiate

the seriousness of the event and the necessity for the procedure. He informed me, "Now, you can resume your exercise whenever you feel like you are able. Just do not overexert yourself. Take it easy for a while and listen to your body."

My hearth cath was on Monday. The following Friday, I started my gradual recovery and began jogging again on a limited basis until I could reach full speed. That was 24 years ago.

God apparently had something else in store for me. He reminded me of my mortality and of the fragility of our human condition. I was mortal after all! If Abraham Lincoln, George Washington, or even President Kennedy had to die, what was so special about me? Why should I be exempt from death? One moment we are here, and the next we may be gone. God, however, had given me a rather obvious message. It was not yet a stop sign, but He cautioned me I to slow down, smell the roses, and remember that God, not Denny Bonner, is in charge.

Ecclesiastes 3:1-2: *There is a time for everything, and a season for every activity under heaven: a time to be born and a time to die.* (NIV)

CHAPTER 33

INFANTS IN CHRIST

Hebrews 5:13: *Anyone who lives on milk, being still an infant, is not acquainted with the teaching about righteousness. But solid food is for the mature, who by constant use have trained themselves to distinguish good from evil.* (NIV)

As a newly married couple, Donna and I truly were mere infants in Christ when we moved back to Kentucky, specifically to Lexington, from Lewisburg, Ohio, in May 1969. We promptly joined Gardenside Baptist Church on Alexandria Drive, where both of us sang in the sanctuary choir and jointly taught the senior high school church training youth group for several years. We were the leaders for the Alpha Teens study group and served as volunteer youth ministers. I also initially taught a young-men's Sunday school class and was ordained a Baptist deacon there, serving under several well reputed Christian mentors. I later taught a young couples' Sunday school class and was a member of the pastoral search committee that called the new pastor, as well.

Donna was actively involved in the music program,

serving both as youth choir director and as an occasional interim minister of music. Even though both of us had grown up in the church, she at White Lick Baptist Church in Berea and me at Christian Baptist Church in Vanceburg, Gardenside Baptist launched us on that joint spiritual journey that is continuing over 50 years later. We have very fond memories of our years at Gardenside Baptist Church, years, which teem with poignant, often humorous, and lasting memories.

We moved our church membership from Gardenside Baptist to Calvary Baptist Church on High Street, Lexington, in 1979, mainly because Donna had tremendous appreciation for the music program at Calvary and a very deep sense of respect and admiration for Ruth Fife, the Minister of Music. Here, as a couple, we taught a joint Sunday school class in the Calvary Baptist College Department; sang in the sanctuary choir; and served on several leadership committees within the church. Donna was ordained as a deacon at Calvary and served several extensive terms as interim Minister of Music. I served as vice-chairman of the deacons and again became an elected member a of a pastoral search committee, this time seeking out a new pastor for Calvary Baptist Church in Lexington.

Our 20 years at Calvary are almost a blur because they passed so quickly. Both our children, Tracey and Amanda, grew up at Calvary and became Christians. Calvary witnessed the baptisms of both daughters, and many wonderful, caring people nurtured them in their spiritual development. We still relish the abundance of wonderful Christian friends and spiritual memories that accompany any reminiscences of Calvary.

I sincerely believe God had been preparing us for 30 years when another church contacted Donna to become interim Minister of Music in the spring of 1999. Loving and compassionate Christian mentors, both at Gardenside Baptist Church and Calvary Baptist Church, studying God's holy word, and teaching and serving His children had hopefully weened us spiritual infants from milk and prepared us for more solid spiritual food.

CHAPTER 34

THE FRUIT OF THE SPIRIT

Galatians 5:22: *But the fruit of the Spirit is love, joy, peace, patience, kindness, faithfulness, gentleness, and self-control. Against such things there is no law.* (NIV)

Donna and I were active members of Calvary Baptist Church in 1999, when the chairperson of a choral search committee at another church first contacted Donna about the possibility of serving as interim minister of music. Since I was still teaching in the College Department of Calvary Baptist at the time, she decided to make a solo visit to the Sunday morning service to see what the church looked like and to "scout out" the situation. The report she shared after that visit was not exactly encouraging.

"The congregation primarily consists of an aging membership," she reported. "I don't think I would be a very good fit for them or me. First, the quality of the musicians is very suspect with very little talent as best I can see. It is a typical untrained church choir. There is not much room for improvement. In addition, I do not believe this congregation would be very receptive to having a woman as a minister of music, even on an interim basis. They appear to be very conservative. I would just not be a very good fit."

The door seemed closed to her.

Several weeks passed, and Donna did not expect to hear anything further from committee. Then, she received a phone call from the chairperson of the committee.

"The committee and the pastor would like to meet with you about our position. Would you be interested in meeting with the committee?" he asked.

"Well, I'll meet with the committee," she explained, "but remember I am still a full-time choral music teacher at Dunbar High School, and I am not looking for another job."

"It is only a part time interim position," he assured her. "At least meet with us and see what we have to say."

"Let me pray about it," Donna requested, "and I will get back to you."

During the next several days, three or four people on the committee called her to encourage her to consider, so she somewhat reluctantly agreed to meet with the committee, not anticipating that she would be even remotely interested.

During the ensuing meeting, Donna asked both the pastor and the committee point black, "Will anyone have any trouble with a woman in the pulpit? If so, I will not consider this any further. I have been in churches before where problems arose over this issue, and I certainly do not want to cause any problem in this church."

"There might be one or two who would have some reservations, but I have found this church to be very receptive to change, and I believe they will embrace you," the pastor assured her.

Donna agreed to pray further about the situation, and several weeks later agreed to become minister of music on a part time interim basis. She had been on the job less than a month when the pastor again approached her.

"The people of this congregation seem to like you a great deal since you have come on board. Since it is only part time anyway, and since you are doing the work anyway, why don't we just take off the term *interim*, and you can continue to serve as minister of music indefinitely?" he proposed.

Thus, Donna became the minister of music at a church where she and I would serve joyfully and faithfully for nearly 11 years. She injected a new energy into the music program that became contagious to the entire church. The sanctuary choir grew in number, she resurrected and directed the hand-bell choir, and she formed both an all-ladies' vocal ensemble group and a men's gospel quartet to provide a variety of music for the Sunday services. She also enlisted regular guest soloists and other gifted musicians to give some spice and variety to the worship services. Under her leadership, with some assistance from me as the newly elected choir president, we began having annual choir retreats to kick off the Christmas season and to begin work on the Christmas music. In short, the music program flourished and blossomed. She and I even voluntarily assumed the responsibility of doing hospital visitation for two years while the church was without a pastor after the previous pastor retired. She did all of this with very minimal increases in compensation.

I also became actively involved in the life of the church. During that 11-year period, I served every year but one as a deacon, served as both vice-chairperson and chairperson of the deacons, and served as choir president for 9 of the 11 years. In addition, I taught a mixed couples Sunday School class for 10 years, served on both the music committee and the personnel committee, supervised the revision of the constitution and bylaws, and voluntarily greeted those who attended the 8:15 a.m. Sunday morning service for a two-year term when the church was under the leadership of an interim pastor. I also chaired the search committee responsible for calling a new minister of education, as well as the hospital visitation committee.

In short, Donna and I really felt God called us to that church. We sensed his presence in our lives through the Holy Spirit while we were there, and we served loyally the entire time we were there. God truly blessed our ministry there.

Before I retired from teaching language arts at Lafayette Senior High School, I was captivated one day by a poster attached to a fellow teacher's door. Not intended to be religious in nature at all, it seemed to me to be a very profound and poignant statement about what should be our condition as Christians. It simply said, "The only sign of life is Growth!"

If we are not growing as Christians, can we really be alive? I think not.

Donna and I grew and matured spiritually, and I believe the church prospered while we were there. Even though there were times when we had lapses in our faith and lapses in our service to God and the church, as all of us do, we really tried to live by displaying, in our lives, the fruit of the spirit as delineated by the apostle Paul in the opening scripture passage of this chapter.

Beware, however! Just when we are experiencing our greatest moments and providing our greatest service for God, Satan often will try to bring it all crashing down.

I Peter 5: 8-9: *Be self-controlled and alert. Your enemy the devil prowls around like a roaring lion looking for someone to devour. Resist him, standing firm in your faith.* (NIV)

CHAPTER 35

BIBLICAL MEN OF FAITH (AND WEAKNESS)

I John 1:8: *If we claim to be without sin, we deceive ourselves and the truth is not in us. If we confess our sins, he is faithful and just and will forgive our sins and purify us from all unrighteousness. If we claim we have not sinned, we make him out to be a liar and his word has no place in our lives.* (NIV)

I have been a student of the *Bible* for almost my entire adult life and let me be very quick to acknowledge that God always has used, and still uses flawed, sinful people to implement and carry out His lofty and holy mission. Both the *Old Testament* and *New Testament* are replete with such people. They were people who sometimes failed at most inopportune times, often when God needed them the most. Yet, at other times, they ascended to magnificent spiritual heights in their quest to follow God. Examples are numerous.

Judah, one of Joseph's brothers, was one such Old Testament character. Perhaps you remember the story of how Judah deceived his daughter-in-law, after the deaths of her two husbands (two of his sons) and denied her the opportunity to conceive an heir through the third son. In revenge, she deceitfully disguised herself as a prostitute, seduced her own father-in-law, Judah, and conceived a son through him. Judah, who then was guilty of committing adultery with his own daughter-in-law, later confessed his sin in Genesis 38:26. Surprisingly, God eventually chose his tribe from among the twelve tribes of Israel to be the one through which Jesus Christ would be born of a virgin in Bethlehem. Is it not amazing that an incestuous adulterer would provide the bloodline for Jesus?

More familiar to us, perhaps, is another Old Testament character, King David. God empowered the prophet Samuel to anoint David as king of Israel. Yet, in a moment of weakness and temptation, David's sinful desire resulted in both adultery and murder. He viewed the naked Bathsheba from his balcony, lusted for her, invited her to his chambers, seduced her, conceived a child with her, and ordered her husband Uriah into battle and ordered him murdered so he could cover up his sinful deed. Failing to recognize his sinfulness and guilt, David could experience reconciliation only when the prophet Nathaniel revealed David's sin to him. Psalms 51:10 reveals King David's heartfelt plea for forgiveness and restoration:

> *Create in me a clean heart, O God; and renew a right spirit within me. Cast me not away from thy presence: and take not thy holy spirit from me. Restore unto me the joy of thy salvation: and uphold me with thy free spirit. Then will*

> *I teach transgressors thy way, and sinners shall
> be converted unto thee.* (KJV)

God heard David's cry and restored him. In fact, David became an ancestor of Jesus, noted in Mathew *1:1* as the "son of David," and David became "a man after God's own heart." (Acts 13:22)

Paul, as noted in Acts, spent his early years stalking, persecuting, and executing Christians. In fact, Paul was on the scene, supervising the situation, when Stephen was stoned to death. God stuck Paul blind, however, during his miraculous conversion on the Road to Damascus in Acts 9. Subsequently, and arguably, Paul became the greatest missionary the world has ever known. He was almost singlehandedly responsible for spreading the Gospel to the entire Gentile world in the first century A.D. Paul is responsible for writing at least 13 books of the 32 books in the New Testament. If he wrote the book of "Hebrews," which many Biblical scholars believe, then he would have written 14 books of the New Testament's 27 books, over half of the New Testament books. He was another everyday ordinary saint.

Therefore, there is no doubt that God has used, and always will use, flawed sinful people to accomplish His will. This means He can use us too. In fact, if He has only human beings to work with, does He really have any other choice? God can and does use flawed and sinful people in miraculous ways when they repent and turn from their sinful ways.

On the other hand, some people who claim to be godly, at times, are not so godly after all and will never be godly unless they experience changed hearts. We have witnessed their existence in the front-page newspaper headlines of the *Lexington Herald Leader* or *New York Times:* names such as Jim Jones, David Koresh, Charles Manson, Jim Baker, and Jimmy Swaggart, to name a few. Some of them, supposedly in the name of Jesus, have done irreparable damage to the Christian community and to the Christian church. These men and women temporarily submitted their lives to the influence of Satan.

2 Corinthians 11:13: *. . . such men are false apostles, deceitful workmen, masquerading as apostles of Christ. And no wonder, for Satan himself masquerades as an angel of light. It is not surprising, then, if his servants masquerade as servants of righteousness. Their ending will be what their actions deserve.* (NIV)

CHAPTER 36

OF PSYCHIC MONSTERS
AND MALFORMED

At the beginning of Chapter 8 of his epic novel *East of Eden*, John Steinbeck philosophizes about the nature of human beings just before we meet Kathy, the evil villainous heroine of the novel, for the first time:

> "I believe there are monsters born in the world to human parents. Some you can see, misshapen and horrible, with huge heads or tiny bodies: some are born with no arms, no legs, some with three arms, some with tails or mouths in odd places. They are accidents and no one's fault, as used to be thought. Once they were considered the visible punishment for concealed sins.
>
> And just as there are physical monsters, can there not be mental or psychic monsters born? The face and body may be perfect,

but if a twisted gene or a malformed egg
can produce physical monsters, may not the
same process produce a malformed soul?"

Though Donna and I did not know it at the time, we met one such "malformed soul" for the first time when the pastor search committee, previously mentioned in chapter 33, invited a potential minister to preach a trial sermon.

The common practice in most Southern Baptist churches is to have a potential pastor first deliver a trial sermon. Then, after hearing him, if the church vote decrees, the members either extend a "call" for the candidate to become pastor, or the two parties decide they are not a good fit for each other and go their separate ways. In this case, everyone agreed, and a new pastor was "called."

Since Donna had been at the church for a little over 10 years, at first, the new pastor relied very heavily on her for advice. In fact, he wrote of his support for her:

"Thank you for the pleasant disposition and cooperative spirit.

I am excited about working with you.

> I appreciate your competence in music
> and your commitment to ministry. It is an
> honor for me to be a co-laborer with you
> in the kingdom of God. I look forward to
> ministering with you in the years ahead."

The first indication of any potential problem concerning the new minister came in a Facebook message to Donna, dated a few months later. It read as follows:

"We are praying for you and your church. Your new minister destroyed our church. The man did not speak any truth during his short time with us. he divided a church and did nothing to save it. he tore down everything we were doing. he brought a message Sunday am, pm and Wednesday pm...but nothing else. we are trying to forgive him, but it has been very hard... but we will never forget what he has done. please double check his references...watch what he spends... and watch and listen to him as he will say one thing and tell someone else another then play everyone against each other. this church which was growing before he came is now slowly dying. it breaks our hearts. we don't want this to happen to another church."
(Robert Bob)

At first, Donna and I thought the letter was bogus because of the mechanical and grammatical errors (Remember, I am a retired English teacher.) and the obviously fictitious name of the sender. However, the more she thought about it, the more she decided to hand it over to the chairperson of the committee that had called the new minister. This person then took the letter to the preacher and showed it to him.

"I know exactly who this is." He responded. "He is simply a disgruntled former church member. If you know anything about churches, you know that pastors often make enemies. It happens in every church. I assure you that this is nothing more than that."

The chairperson of the committee reported to Donna what seemed a logical explanation, and the Facebook message seemed to fade in importance.

The next episode occurred sometime later when the minister invited Donna into his office between the 8:15 and 10:15 services to have prayer before the second service. He wanted to hold her hand while they prayed, which seemed innocent enough, but then he promptly put his arm around her waist and held her "too tightly," as she described it, while they prayed. Donna was very uncomfortable about the entire experience and vowed she never to be caught in this set of circumstances again. She avoided being alone with him in any circumstance from that day forward and made herself unavailable for any future "prayer meetings." The tension increased.

"It just did not feel right." She would tell me later. She, in fact, hesitated to tell me, her husband, until almost a month later about the experience.

From that point on, things very rapidly deteriorated. Donna talked to the chairman of the deacons and the chairman of the committee that had called him about the unwanted inappropriate touching and other things that were happening, and these two men made an agreement not to leave Donna by herself at anytime, even when she went to the choir room to select music for the choir. The personnel committee gave her permission to avoid the church office except when her duties required her to be there for the weekly staff meetings. Even then, one of those two men would be there to see that nothing further happened; and even though she was required to attend the weekly staff meetings, the chairman of the deacons was also a staff member so he would be there to protect in that environment.

Several other episodes occurred to heighten the tension in the next several months. In one such incident, the minister called Donna and the church secretary (Donna would not go into his office by herself.) into his office. In that meeting, he lambasted my wife for "overt" support of a young man who was owner and operator of a local lawn service company. He had submitted a proposal to maintain the landscape and exterior of the church by mowing and trimming the shrubbery during the summer months and to clean snow and ice from the premises in the winter months. Donna had encouraged him because he was her former student in chorus at Dunbar Senior High School and because he had a beautiful tenor voice. He had begun singing in the sanctuary choir and in the men's gospel quartet that Donna had started as one of her areas of ministry at the church. In fact, he had even become a regular member of my Sunday school class. Though he had made some wrong choices in life, he was becoming involved in a church on a regular basis for the first time in several years.

"There is no hope for that boy!" exclaimed the pastor during the meeting. From that moment, the pastor plotted and schemed to undercut him in any way he could.

At the time when these events were transpiring, I was involved in several areas of leadership in the church. During the two-year interim period when we were without a pastor, I had volunteered to serve as a greeter for the 8:15 service, to assist the interim pastor, and I continued this practice even after the new minister came. In this capacity, I thought I might be of service to him since he was new to the congregation. I reasoned that I could assist him in getting to know the congregation. In addition, I also taught a young couple's Sunday school class and was a member of the board of deacons, as well as chairperson of both the Constitution and By-laws Committee and the Hospital Visitation Committee at the church. I believe my involvement in all these committees is what led to the next confrontation.

I had previously invited the chaplain of Central Baptist Hospital to conduct an in-service training session for my hospital visitation committee, and one of her suggestions was a "goody bag" for any church member who became a patient for an overnight stay in one of the local hospitals. The bag included such items as a toothbrush, a miniature bottle of mouthwash, a roll of breath mints, a tube of lip balm, a small tablet on which a guest could write a small note or phone number, an ink pen, and a copy of *Open Windows,* a daily devotional guide. Some of the older ladies in the church, good seamstresses, agreed to sew together cloth bags with handles in which all the "goodies" could be secured. These bags became very popular items. In fact, my committee was sometimes criticized because we only gave the bags to patients who stayed overnight in the hospital.

On one occasion, the church had several members who were in the hospital, so I secured the key from my wife Donna, entered her music office, and began stuffing hospital bags. The pastor entered the room.

"I am tired of this power struggle," he blurted out, suggesting that Donna and I posed a problem.

Puzzled, I responded, "There is no power struggle."

Other comments were made, many of which I do not remember because of the heat of the moment, but I realized I was getting very angry and decided it would be best for me to leave before I could say something I might later regret, so I turned toward the door to leave the room. The pastor was blocking the door.

"I am so tired of this ego trip!" he exclaimed.

Again, I calmly asserted, "There is no ego trip. I need to leave." He could see that I was becoming very angry through the tone of my voice

"Let's go into my office and discuss this," he proposed.

"I don't want to go into your office to discuss anything!" I retorted.

I was too nervous and too angry to discuss anything at this point. I just wanted to get out of the office without too much confrontation. I brushed my way past him on my way to the main door of the office complex, but not before he could launch his final salvo.

"You are a liar!" he exclaimed as I opened the door and walked into the hallway.

I was hurt and crushed.

"What had I done wrong? What had I done to irritate him? Did he really think I was in a power struggle with him? Is it possible I could really be on an ego trip? Had I been selfish in what I was doing? What could possibly have triggered this? What had I supposedly lied about?"

I doubted my own motives and the nature of all the things I had done for the entire weekend. Donna and I relived the episodes repeatedly, and Donna finally suggested a possible answer to the puzzle.

"You were simply collateral damage," she explained. "He was really trying to get to you through me."

The following Monday, I submitted my resignation from all the committees with which I was affiliated, but I did continue to support Donna by singing in the sanctuary choir and in the gospel music quartet. After 10 years of faithful service to God, the church, and two other ministers, my term of leadership at this church had come to a disappointing end.

CHAPTER 37

THE AGONIZED DECISION

After the confrontation in the music office, Donna and I decided that we needed to meet with someone in a higher position in the church to try to resolve the issues. She could not perform her responsibilities in the church adequately with all the tension and inner turmoil she was experiencing. People in the church were even questioning her about her behavior.

"Are you feeling well?" they asked. "You don't act like your normal happy self. Is something wrong?"

Donna responded, "I have not been sleeping very well at night. I am just very tired. That's all."

"Are you sure you are alright?" they continued to query her.

It was very true. She and I were having a very difficult time sleeping at night because the constant worry and concern were keeping us awake. Sometimes we did not go to sleep until 2:00 or 3:00 in the morning. At other times, we would awaken in the middle of the night. Sometimes, we would even awaken at 4:00 or 5:00 a.m., unable to go back to sleep. On a couple of occasions, we "opened" Cracker Barrel Restaurant at Brannon Crossing in Lexington at 6:00 a.m. We became their first customers of the day. One night, we even "broke out" a bottle of Donna's cooking wine to see if that would help us sleep.

During those times, we often speculated about our plight.

> "What could we have possibly done to precipitate such apparent animosity toward us? Things had started well. Did the conflict start with the Facebook message we had shared, or did it begin with Donna's apparent coolness after the "prayer meeting" encounter? Did she offend the pastor by her apparent rebellion against his advances to her? Was he jealous of my hospital visitation committee because I had often visited the hospital patients before he did? Sometimes, I had already given them their goody bags when he arrived. Was I tying to do too much in the church and appearing to be too egocentric? Was he in some way jealous of us? How was this going to end up? What would happen if the church became aware of what was going on? Would we cause a church split If Donna resigned as minister of music? Would that resolve the situation or intensify it?

We had already experienced one church split and knew the devastating effects of such an outcome. That was the last thing we wanted to happen. The conflict was also affecting the health of both of us. Donna had developed a very painful case of shingles, and for the first time in my life, my family doctor prescribed a hypertension medication for my newly diagnosed high blood pressure.

In desperation, we approached the chairperson of the board of deacons and the chairperson of the personnel committee and informed them of the urgency of the situation. They scheduled a meeting to try to resolve the conflict. The pastor would also attend. There were actually two meetings. One meeting was with Donna *only*, followed by a second meeting which involved me.

Everyone left these meetings feeling more positive about all the issues, the meetings concluded with apologies, and everyone agreed to try to be more sensitive to each other. Donna agreed that she would "hang in there for a while" and give time to allow for healing to take place, even though that would be very difficult.

"You will need to be patient with me," she affirmed. "It might take a while."

Everyone agreed to put forth their best effort

Three weeks after the previous mediation meetings, in front of the rest of the staff in a regularly scheduled staff meeting, the pastor called Donna "belligerent" and exclaimed she was having a "toxic effect on the church." This probably resulted from the fact that some choir members had now become aware of the conflict and had voluntarily stopped attending the Sunday evening service and the Wednesday night prayer meeting service. They came only to choir.

"This is called boycotting," she was told, "and it is snowballing."

He even questioned her musicianship. "Are you a professional?"

Her response was that she was not a professional if he was referring to her having seminary training, but that she had been a professional choral musician nearly all her life in both public education and in church music. She explained that she began playing the piano in church when she was in elementary school and was a choral music director with nearly 40 years of experience in public education choral music, heading one of the largest, most prestigious choral music programs in the state at Dunbar Senior High School, until her retirement two years prior. In addition, she explained, that she had served as interim minister of music on several occasions for both Gardenside Baptist Church and Calvary Baptist Church in Lexington.

"Something has got to give!" the pastor blurted out. "You know we can hire a replacement for you any time. You need to get up in front of the church and tell the truth!"

He even quoted scripture, "The truth will make you free!"

Donna cried throughout most of the rest of the meeting and left the meeting more convinced than ever that she needed either to resign or to ask for a leave of absence. Surprisingly, only one person in the staff meeting, the chairperson of the deacons, came to her defense. Perhaps they were too surprised, shocked, or intimidated to respond.

One month later, since there had been absolutely no effort, phone calls, or any other move toward any form of reconciliation by the pastor, Donna submitted a letter to the personnel committee requesting a three-month leave of absence, to become effective June 30, 2010. This would enable the church to address and rectify the tense situation within the church and would allow Donna some time to relax a little and to escape the daily stress she was feeling, perhaps even get some sleep. She asked, however, that this request not be made publicly known until she had had an opportunity to talk to the choir and tell them about her request. A pastor/mentor friend had advised her that she should tell the choir the truth, or they would be devastated. However, he also issued a word of warning.

"You realize that may not be able to return. You need to be prepared to walk away," he warned.

"I know that" Donna responded, "but if this is the way it is going to be, I really don't want to be here anyway. Even though I love music and the people of the church, this not good for my health."

Donna shared the announcement with the choir at the next Wednesday evening rehearsal

The personnel committee, however, requested that, because of the short notice, in order not to leave the music program and choir "hanging," she should lead the choir and congregation as normal on the following Sunday. The personnel committee also indicated that it would not be good for Donna simply to disappear without any explanation. They would read a public announcement to the congregation at the end of both morning services. Donna agreed to those terms, even though it was very difficult to attend the next Sunday, especially since the choir and the pastor already knew what the announcement would be.

The following Wednesday, during a regular business meeting, after a great deal of discussion, the church membership voted not to allow Donna a leave of absence; they had been hoodwinked by the pastor into voting for an issue that did not even require church approval. This was supposed to have been strictly a personnel committee responsibility. We later learned that the pastor had recruited several of his allies to attend the meeting so that they could vote down the request, and that Donna's request was tendered against a "stacked deck." He clearly wanted her to resign. Many of the members of the congregation "drank the poisoned Kool Aid" just as surely as did the over 900 members of Jim Jones' church, who died in a South African jungle in Guyana on November 18,1978. Donna's choice then became obvious; she could report to the tremendously uncomfortable church office atmosphere as usual, or she could choose not to return at all.

The next day, Donna submitted her letter of resignation as minister of music. The pastor had managed to negate and destroy her 10-year ministry in only nine months, the amount of time needed to conceive a baby. He, however, had conceived innumerable lies, cunning deceit, and an extremely divided church.

Matthew 7:13-20 reminds us of such people:

> *"Watch out for false prophets. They come to you in sheep's clothing, but inwardly they*

are ferocious wolves. By their fruits you will recognize them. Do people pick grapes from thorn bushes, or figs from thistles? Likewise every good tree bears good fruit, but a bad tree bears bad fruit. A good tree cannot bear bad fruit, and a bad tree cannot bear good fruit. Every tree that does not bear good fruit is cut down and thrown into the fire. Thus, by their fruit you will recognize them." (NIV)

Donna and I have discovered, since we left that church, that previous churches suffered similarly. One necessitated visitation by a state Baptist mediation team and ended up with a split, and the other church split within his first year as pastor there.

Three years later, two and one-half years after Donna and I had removed our membership from the church, the deacons requested and accepted his resignation as pastor. He became the pastor of another small rural church, even though officials in the Elkhorn Association of Kentucky Southern Baptist Convention had informed them of what had happened. Again, the new church "drank the poison Kool Aid." Just this past fall, we learned that this minister was also asked to resign from that church as well. He now has destroyed four churches with his hypocritical and deceptive ministry.

I often speculate about how many churches and how many good Christian lives have been destroyed during his hypocritical ministry. Just as surely as he ripped our church and ministry from beneath our feet, he has done so for many others. I pray for him every day during my devotional time that he will repent and mend his ways before he meets his Maker at the Pearly Gates. I pity him if he is accountable to God for his previous actions.

Is it any wonder that so many people, particularly the younger generation, have become alienated from organized church worship?

CHAPTER 38

GOSSIP GALORE

Following Donna's resignation, we found it very difficult to attend church anywhere for some time. We had previously attended several churches in Lexington and were fortunate to have garnered many good Christian friends in our Christian pilgrimage, but this was somewhat of a handicap in a way. In every church we visited, our situation became sensitive because we inevitably met someone we knew, had to explain discreetly what had happened, and had to do so without trashing someone else or appearing to be gossips. It was sometimes easier just to stay home on Sunday, watch a church service on TV, and not have to explain to anyone why we were no longer in our home church. We were churchless for the first time in over 40 years.

Another problem that resulted from our voluntary departure from the Church was that we had made ourselves so vulnerable to verbal attacks, slander, and defamation from the pastor and his friends. The rumors were rampant! They could say whatever they wanted to say, and we were not there to defend ourselves. One such incident occurred on the campus of Georgetown College.

It happened when the former pastor approached a good friend and mentor who had worked with Donna as interim pastor at that same church for two years while we were seeking a full-time pastor. His wife, chief chaplain for Central Baptist Hospital in Lexington, was with him. They had traveled from Frankfort to Georgetown College to attend the dedicatory ceremony of the new office of Baptist Seminary of Lexington. That afternoon, I received the following email message from my friend:

"I saw the new pastor today and he said some very disturbing things. He said he 'had to get rid of the Bonners.' He made additional comments that were very inappropriate. I was shocked and saddened by his words. Let me know if there is anything I can do for you and Donna."

I immediately called him, briefly brought him up to date on everything that had happened, and he invited us to his home to explain what had been said to him at Georgetown College.

"I don't want to discuss it on the phone," he stated. "I would rather talk to you and Donna personally."

We arranged a time and went to his home in Frankfort to meet with him. He had prepared coffee and refreshments for us when we arrived. What a compassionate and loving man he was. He repeated the contents of the entire conversation he and his wife had had with the former pastor. The following were among some of the statements made during the conversation:

"Hello. This is my wife." He apparently opened the conversation.

"Hey. Yes, you were at the church before me," he stated.

"I just have one question," our friend queried. "Are you still having Sunday night services?"

"Yes, we are. Why do you ask?

"That one thing tells me a lot about how things are going at the church. How are things going?"

"Good. I had to get rid of the Bonners," the former pastor responded.

"Really?" he responded.

"Yes, I had lots of trouble with them, the former pastor responded. "I believe that Denny is seriously mentally ill. Did you have any trouble with the Bonners?" the pastor queried.

"No. We had no troubles. We got along fine."

"I really do believe that Denny has some serious mental illness," the former pastor responded.

"Have you lost a lot of church members because of the departure of the Bonners?" asked John.

"Just a few; perhaps three or four," he confessed. He pressed the question, "So the Bonners gave you no trouble while you were at Concord Baptist Church?"

"None. We got along fine. Well, we had better go in."

At this point, the service was beginning inside, and they had to cut short the conversation.

This was but one of the many slanderous statements made after we left the church. One rumor was that Donna had been fired from her last job as choral music director and music teacher at Dunbar Senior High School. She had taught almost 40 years in the Fayette County Public Schools. In addition, the Kentucky Music Educators formally honored and recognized her as the "Outstanding Senior High School Music Teacher of the Year," but the rumor was that she was supposedly fired from her Job.

James 3:5-10: *"Likewise the tongue is a small part of the body, buy it makes great boasts. Consider what a great forest is set on fire by a small spark. The tongue is also a fire, a world of evil among the parts of the body. It corrupts the whole person, sets the whole course of his life on fire, and is itself set on fire by hell. All kinds of animal, birds, reptiles and creatures of the sea are being tamed and have been tamed by man, but no man can tame the tongue. It is a restless evil, full of deadly poison. With the tongue we praise our Lord and Father, and with it we curse men, who have been made in God's likeness. Out of the same mouth come praise and cursing. My brothers, this should not be."* (NIV)

CHAPTER 39

THE OUTSIDERS

"Why don't we just take a vacation and get out of town for a while," Donna suggested. "Not only would that allow us to get away, but it would also keep us from having to explain things to people and from having to listen to all the rumors. Since we have had to plan everything around Wednesday nights and Sunday services for several years, we have not been able to enjoy a real vacation. Maybe that would allow us a little time to recover."

It was true. We had sacrificed most of our time to focusing on church commitments and had not really had an opportunity to enjoy free time with each other. Our highly regimented church schedule had imprisoned us in a way. Our social life, of necessity, had been sandwiched either between Sunday evening worship services and Wednesday night choir practices or between Wednesday evening choir practices and early Sunday morning worship services. Though we had been actively involved in the church all our married life, we were depressed, fatigued, and very disappointed with the established church. We were suffering from what Christian friend, Ira Prosser, once referred to as "churchitis." We were burned out on church.

"Where would you like to go?" I queried.

"Well, we enjoy visiting New York City and going to Broadway shows," Donna suggested. "Perhaps we should just go to New York City for a week or so. Or we could just spend some time lying on the beach, reading, and soaking up the sun in Myrtle Beach, South Carolina, or Hilton Head."

We had already savored many of the amenities of Myrtle Beach with our good friends, H. S. and Linda Yarborough, when he served as Minister of Music at Calvary Baptist Church. For two or three years in a row, he had arranged for some members of the Calvary youth choir to attend the "Sonshine Music Festival" in Myrtle Beach, and we had served as chaperones for that event.

"Maybe we should just drive to California and see Tracey," she surmised. "We certainly can take all the time we want. We could even go through Oklahoma City and visit Amanda and J. D. or perhaps visit my Aunt Bonnie in Albuquerque."

Consequently, we hatched plans for the infamous Bonner two week 3,800-mile odyssey to Laguna Nigel, California, in August 2010. Our trip included a stop at the Corvette Museum in Bowling Green, KY, and a 2 day stay in Memphis, Tennessee. We visited Graceland, meandered through the streets of the musical district of Memphis, witnessed the march of the ducks at the historical Peabody Hotel, and spent nearly an entire day reliving the last moments of Dr. Martin Luther King's life and touring the Civil Rights Museum. In fact, we celebrated our 45th wedding anniversary by savoring the southern cuisine of the Peabody Hotel restaurant.

It was a very welcome relief from the stress we had experienced because of the traumatizing events. The more we were able to distance ourselves from Lexington, the more we were able to relax and enjoy our lives together again. We were having a honeymoon experience 45 years after the original event.

Our next stop was Oklahoma City and a visit with our daughter Amanda and her husband J. D. Church. They had just purchased their first home as newlyweds, so we were able to experience the joy of getting them settled in their new home. Donna cleaned floors and bathrooms, moved furniture in place, and unpacked dishes and silverware, meticulously placing all items in their freshly cleaned permanent locations. I, on the other hand, experienced the wonderful good fortune of assembling what seemed to be thousands of nuts, bolts, screws, and panels into structures that eventually resembled a bookcase and two gigantic corner computer desks. The resulting fatigue was good for us, particularly Donna and me, as we further divorced ourselves from events in Lexington.

Our next stop was Albuquerque, New Mexico, which witnessed Donna's long anticipated reunion with her aunt, Bonnie Welch, and her family, consisting of Bonnie's 4 daughters, their husbands, and all the grand children and great grand children, some of whom we had never met. There were between 30 and 35 people who gathered for the departing cookout and swim party before we departed for Flagstaff, Arizona, the next day. It was wonderful to bask in and drink in the warm fellowship of precious family members, recalling funny long forgotten stories and memories and becoming inebriated with the joy, love, and unfettered acceptance lavished upon us. Tracey also flew from California to Albuquerque, partially to spring a surprise visit on Bonnie and partially to accompany us for the remainder of the trip to California.

At a rest stop, on the way down the winding, canyon road into Sedona, we received the seemingly inconsequential phone call from a dear friend, a member of our former church. Many of our dearest Christian friends from the church knew in advance of our plans to escape Lexington for a while and knew we were travelling to California to visit Tracey for a few days. She was checking on us.

"Donna, where are you all?" she curiously prodded.

"We are travelling down the winding canyon road into Sedona," Donna responded. "We decided to take the scenic rural route instead of the interstate highway, and the scenery is gorgeous! We are going to spend the afternoon in Sedona, then go back to Flagstaff to spend the night there. Tomorrow we are then heading out to the Grand Canyon on our way into Las Vegas.

"It sounds like you all are having a wonderful time," she surmised. "I wish I could be there with you."

"We really are," Donna replied. "We wish you could be here too. We are also going to visit Hoover Dam and Lake Mead on the way into Las Vegas. We will probably spend at least one day in Vegas before finally heading into Laguna Nigel," Donna reported.

Viewed in retrospect, that phone call would become

very providential in nature and would provide another much-needed boost to our severely damaged and fragile spiritual egos.

"My husband and I want to have a cookout when you get back. We would love to see all the pictures you have taken and just spend some time with you guys." she suggested. "We love you guys and miss you so much."

"We love you too, and thanks for calling to check on us. That sounds like a wonderful idea." Donna responded.

"We will be glad to have it at our house," she offered. "My husband and I will make some phone calls and invite some of our other church friends. It will be great to get together and see you guys again."

Thus, was conceived a reunion party, that would grow to incorporate nearly 30 former church members. Our group would multiply to include 4 former deacon chairmen, as well as several deacons, choir members, and Sunday school teachers. Our retired pastor, under whom Donna had served as Minister of Music even became a part of the group.

Someone in the group once remarked, "We can start our own church."

However, that was never the intent of our get together. We simply loved being together again.

Even now, nearly 14 years later, as we have separated, scattered, and moved our memberships to various churches around Lexington, we still love and enjoy each other so much that we continue to meet once a month. We have dubbed ourselves "The Outsiders" because we are "outside" the fellowship of our former church. Each month, we enjoy a fellowship meal and have a time of reflection and prayer to end our meeting.

Someone recently remarked about our meeting, "This is really church as far as I am concerned."

The group has served as a wonderful support group for Donna and me and has helped heal the spiritual void and despair that resulted from traumatic episode in our lives. Members have helped to validate each other in our spiritual journey through what almost seemed to be the equivalent of ". . . the valley of the shadow of death."

Is that not what Christians are supposed to do for each other?

My life and I will never be the same because of the outsiders.

Again, the words of E. Glen Hinson ring so profoundly true, "God doesn't always drive a bulldozer, but he often has a way of hammering question marks into exclamation marks."

Even though there are still some question marks, my life truly has more exclamation marks than question marks.

The scars will always be there, just as will the scars from my bicycle accident on Second Street in Vanceburg 75 years ago. They, however, are not external physical scars, but are instead deep painful mental and psychological ones. We cannot totally erase them and restore the innocence and perfection that once graced our lives; but patience, Christian fellowship, the passage of time, and love can make them less prominent.

Jeremiah 30:17: *For I will restore health unto thee, and I will heal thee of thy wounds, saith the Lord, because they called thee an outcast.* (KJV)

CHAPTER 40

RUMMAGING AND PILFERING

After the anticipated death of Aunt Eula and the unexpected brutal carjacking death of Uncle Bill in early December 1995, my cousin, Rhenda Mills, by default, had to handle the affairs of their entire estate. This posed a serious problem for Rhenda because she was so emotionally fragile, having just experienced the sudden loss of both parents in a little less than two weeks. In addition, serious questions about the uncertainty of her own future health loomed on the horizon because one month later in January 1996, she received a cancer diagnosis, another in the long list of seven malignancies that would plague her for the remainder of her life.

The administration of the Bonner estate, further complicated by a will that granted one half of the estate to Rhenda and the other one half to the remaining four adopted children, whom Uncle Bill and Aunt Eula had legally adopted on June 19, 1964. In addition, Aunt Eula had been a hoarder for most of her married life. There was a lot of stuff.

The enormity of the task challenged Rhenda to the utmost, not only because of the overwhelming emotional trauma she had experienced, but also because of necessity for extremely urgent diplomatic skills that would be needed to maneuver through the entire process. She was simply unable either physically or emotionally to undertake such a monumental task. The result was that she chose to do nothing during the remainder of her lifetime. The Bonner home and the affairs of the estate in Vanceburg remained in limbo for nearly 18 years, until after Rhenda's death on January 17, 2013.

Three months later, in late April 2013, Rhenda's surviving husband, and, by default, "new" executor of the estate of Eula, William, and Rhenda Mills, finally began the process that had first been set in motion by the deaths of Uncle Bill and Aunt Eula in December 1995. He tackled what Rhenda could never have tackled.

Perhaps it was God's will, certainly no accident, that someone other than a Bonner, someone with less emotional and psychological attachment, would be the one who would complete a process that had begun many years earlier.

As mentioned earlier, Aunt Eula was a hoarder in the classic sense of the word. For her, it was almost impossible for her to pass a garage sale or yard sale without some purchase of some kind: something that they might one day need. Most of this treasure had been stored in the house, stacked from floor to ceiling with simply a path through each room. Compound all of that with the added furniture salvaged from Mom's house when she passed away and from Boot's estate as well. Even the front porch was jam packed with assorted cabinets, chairs, clothing, boxes, golf clubs, and patio furniture.

In fact, when the house on Second Street became impassable, Aunt Eula and Uncle Bill stored items in several other buildings around town as they ran out of room. They even purchased my mother's property on South Fairlane Drive, simply to have a place to sleep, when I had to seek another private facility for my mother. You can image the complexity of trying to sort through all these items! Perhaps this is another reason why Rhenda refused to undertake the monumental task.

A further complication resulted from the fact that the property had apparently been broken into, vandalized, and trashed several times during the intervening 18 years. A burglar pulled drawers from all the furniture in an apparent search for something of value and indiscriminately scattered the contents throughout the house. Items of known value had disappeared, and the intruders left an almost unfathomable trail of clothing, valuable papers and documents, and monumental piles of momentous and precious keepsake items. The place was truly one of the most shocking scenes I have witnessed during my entire lifetime. Cleanup was a very daunting task at best!

In late April and early May of 2013, Rhenda's husband and I, along with assistance from some family members, began the process of sorting through and discarding items of Aunt Eula and Uncle Bill's private property. Doyle rented a huge dumpster to facilitate the process; and, when we had finished discarding rotting or deteriorated items, over 28,000 pounds of debris and garbage was delivered to the Tollesboro landfill. The remainder, items of value and worth, were auctioned off in Flemingsburg on July 27, 2013.

We spent nearly two weeks rummaging through and pilfering through the lives of Aunt Eula, Uncle Bill, and Rhenda. Sometimes I felt as if I were an alien invader or intruder and certainly had no right whatsoever to be invading their privacy in such a way. One day, the following thought came to me:

> "I wonder if God rummages through our lives to find things of value and worth when our physical existence ceases. Perhaps, just as I discovered with Aunt Eula, Uncle Bill, and Rhenda's treasures, He would find many things of great value. He would perhaps find a set of yearbooks with invaluable intimate inscriptions, ones made by long forgotten dear friends. Perhaps an old, dog-eared photograph of me with a Perry Como cardigan sweater and a flat-top haircut, or perhaps a picture of my brother with his high school prom date. The treasure might include a long-forgotten charcoal drawing of the old Lewis County High School building, now demolished, or perhaps a collection of photographs from the 1937 flood that ravaged Vanceburg. Perhaps, he would discover a priceless set of bronzed baby shoes that belonged to my cousin Burgess,

> a youthful photograph of Mom, a
> yearbook picture of a dark-haired Denny
> Bonner and a high school reminder that I
> had been chosen Mr. Lewis County High
> School in 1959."

These, however, are not the kinds of treasures God would want to find in the memories of my life. He would want to find things of spiritual value, things like a well-worn dilapidated Bible with loose or perhaps even missing pages to show that I regularly visited His word. He would want a record of those people for whom I attempted to provide spiritual depth and growth through a Calvary Baptist Church Sunday School Class or Bible Study Fellowship group study of Genesis or Matthew. In addition, He would remember the much-needed financial gift I gave to a Berea College student in August 2013 or perhaps the loan I provided for my brother when his income did not quite cover the emergency expenses. He might remember the time when I transported a dear pastor friend to Good Samaritan Hospital for a long anticipated "date" with his wife whom he was missing very much. Maybe He would remember the time when I aided the nurses in getting a good friend to the bedpan during the last days of his life at St. Joseph Hospital; or the joy I hopefully brought to someone else's life by encouraging him, providing a shoulder to cry on during a time of crisis or need. These remembrances are the kinds of treasures God looks for when He rummages through the remnants of our lives. I just hope he does not have to rummage through 28,000 pounds of dirt, debris, trash, and mouse droppings to discover something valuable about my life.

Matthew 6:19: *Do not store up for yourselves treasures on earth where moth and rust decay, and where thieves break in and steal. But store up for yourselves treasures in heaven, where moth and rust do not destroy, and where thieves do not break in and steal. For where your treasure is, there your heart will be also.* (NIV)

CHAPTER 41

LIFE IS ONLY A MIST

Our younger daughter, Amanda called around 6:30 or 7:00 pm on Wednesday, Feb 5, 2014, to inform us that she was on the way to Mercy Hospital in Oklahoma City with her husband J. D. Church for what they thought was the flue. He had experienced vomiting, diarrhea, chilling, and intense fever for several days. When they arrived at the hospital, the medical staff immediately admitted him to the intensive care unit and placed him on a ventilator and kidney dialysis machine: definite indicators that it was much more than simply the flue. We told Amanda to keep us informed.

One day later, on Thursday, Feb. 6, around 3:00 in the afternoon, Amanda called Donna to bring her the latest update.

"Mom, I'm scared!" Amanda tearfully proclaimed from the other end of the phone. "J.D coded twice this morning and had to be resuscitated. They have put him on additional life support equipment, and his bodily organs have begun shutting down. They have mentioned a blood infection called sepsis and have started him on very powerful antibiotics. I am really scared!"

Those were the only words needed. Donna and I hurriedly threw a few things together, along with dress clothing, expecting perhaps to have to attend a funeral and embarked on the 14-hour automobile trip to Oklahoma City. We drove all night and arrived about 6:00 a.m. the following morning, Friday, February 7. Amanda was already at the hospital, along with J. D.'s relatives: his mom, dad, sister and aunt, all of whom had flown in from Pittsburgh earlier that morning at the behest of the physicians. The anticipated long wait began. For the next 7 days, Amanda and his family stood watch over her comatose husband.

On Saturday night, Feb 8, Donna and I talked to Amanda about returning to Lexington for a few days and then returning to Oklahoma City later. We anticipated an extended hospital stay, perhaps even a necessary stay in an extended care facility after his release from the hospital. Since his parents were planning to say for as long as they felt the need, we reasoned that we might be needed more urgently later, to relieve them, especially if long-term health care in a special medical facility became a necessity. Amanda, however, tearfully pleaded for us to delay our return until we could see him on Sunday morning.

"Why don't you wait and leave tomorrow morning and see how he is doing tomorrow?" she pleaded.

I believe she was almost convinced that this would be the last time we would see him alive.

We arrived at the intensive care waiting room early on Sunday morning, February 9, visited for a few minutes, said our very tearful goodbye, and began our pilgrimage back to Lexington, interrupted only by an unexpected overnight stay near Evansville, Indiana, during a blinding snowstorm.

We arrived back in Lexington around noon on Monday, February 10. I had responsibilities as a group leader in Bible Study Fellowship on Monday night at 6:50 p.m., and Donna had rehearsal for her Cantabile Vocal Ensemble singing group at 6:30.

Wednesday morning, Feb 12, 6:00 a.m. Amanda called. "Mom, he coded 2 more times last night, the last time around 2:00 a.m. this morning. The doctors say that they will probably not be able to resuscitate him if it happens again."

"Oh, my goodness!" was the only response Donna could muster

Amanda explained further, "The doctors say he probably has had severe heart damage or brain damage. They say we should probably remove him from the ventilator and any additional life support systems."

Amanda had already conversed with his family. "What do you think we should do? I am simply his wife. He is your son."

They looked at each other indecisively before addressing Amanda. "It is up to you, Amanda. You are the one who needs to decide. We are ok with whatever decision you make. He is already gone from that shell of a human being anyway. Doctors cannot do anything else. We do not want to lose our son, but we leave the decision totally up to you. You must decide what is best."

"Well, I guess we need to stop all life support systems and see what happens," Amanda tearfully suggested.

Once the nurses removed the medical support systems, Amanda's husband passed away within 2 or 3 minutes. Ironically, it was just a little over a week until his 34th birthday. He had been in the hospital less than a week. Amanda was a widow at only 34 years of age, just 2 days before Valentine's Day.

The family held a memorial service on Saturday, Feb 15, at 2:00 in Bishop W. Angie Smith Chapel on the campus of Oklahoma City University where they had first met. Amanda now faced a future without her friend, lover, and husband of only 6 years.

She entertained several of his friends for a memorial birthday party, hosted in memory of what would have been his 34th birthday, on Friday, Feb. 21.

Life gives us no guarantee of longevity and often startles us with its "smash mouth" harsh realities.

James 4:13-16: *Now listen, you who say, "Today or tomorrow we will go to this or that city, spend a year there, carry on business and make money." Why you do not even know what will happen tomorrow! What is your life? You are a mist that appears for a little while and then vanishes. Instead, you ought to say, "If it is the Lord's will, we will live and do this or that." As it is, you boast and brag.* (NIV)

I used to pray that God's will would be done in all my daily crises, but I have somewhat tempered that request in recent years as I have witnessed numerous instances of God's will being carried out in miraculous ways during my lifetime. I sincerely believe that God will ultimately accomplish His desire for me anyway because He is God, and I am not. My prayer now is simply that I will be able to accept His will regardless of what that may be.

CHAPTER 42

A LEASE ON LIFE

In October 2003, Donna, Tracey, and I jointly purchased an investment property faithfully speculating that this would be a good source of supplemental income for us and that the property would appreciate with the passing years. So far, even though there have been some expenses involved in maintaining the property, and there have been short periods of time when the property has been vacant, our plan has worked out very well. There have been very few periods of vacancy, we have been able to make the needed repairs, and we are running a good balance in the savings account linked to this property.

Sometimes, however, I am prone to daydream or to "philosophize" during a serendipitous moment of my life, and I experience an epiphany of sorts: my speculation focuses on spiritual thoughts that many people might consider absurd or ridiculous. One such moment occurred when I was recently thinking about our rental property and speculating about God's presence in our lives. You see, our lives are very much like rental property.

First, a rental home is only a temporary dwelling place, and the lessee is generally only going to inhabit the property for a brief period. Often, the lessee will purchase a "real" home or perhaps move into a more elaborate environment with many more of the abundant amenities that life can provide. Our lives are very much like rental homes: our physical existence in a human body is only a temporary one. At death, if we are believers in Jesus, we move on to the eternal, more desirable stage of our existence.

Jesus' words to his disciples in one of the most quoted passages in the *Bible*, addresses the reality of this "new" home. Ministers often recite John 14:1-3 during the funeral of a dear loved one who has passed away. In the passage, Jesus speaks to his disciples about His own impending death, resurrection, departure from them, and His ascension into heaven:

Let not your heart be troubled: ye believe in God, believe also in me. In my Father's house are many mansions; if it were not so, I would have told you. I go to prepare a place for you. And if I go and prepare a place for you, I will come again, and receive you unto myself: that where I am, there you may be also. (KJV)

Obviously, Jesus is referring to Heaven: our perfect, permanent dwelling place with Him, after our earthy home is no longer important. He promises that we will join him there.

One other thing I have learned about rental property is that, when you least expect, you will receive the unwanted telephone call that the gutter is clogged or that either the bathroom or kitchen drain is not working properly. Sometimes it may be a major item such as a replacement furnace, a leaky roof, or a faulty hot water heater. Something always needs repair, maintenance, or expensive replacement.

The same thing is true concerning our everyday lives. How often are our lives interrupted, inconvenienced, and emotionally and tragically altered by unexpected, coincidental events? A job loss, a debilitating automobile accident, depression from severed wedding vows, a life altering divorce, or the birth of a severely handicapped child can wreak havoc on our fragile egos. They too often need assurance and repair. I have discovered that, even during the most gut-retching misfortunes, the *Bible* still offers us hope and peace and can repair our fragile egos.

Jesus explains in Luke 12:27-31:

> *"Consider the lilies how they grow: they toil not, they spin not; and yet I say unto you, that Solomon in all his glory was not arrayed like one of these. If then God so clothe the grass, which is today in the field and tomorrow is cast into the oven; how much more will he clothe you, O thee of little faith? And seek not ye what ye shall eat, or what ye shall drink, neither be ye of a doubtful mind. For all these things do the nations of the world seek after: and your Father knoweth that ye have need of these things. But rather seek ye the kingdom of God; and all these things shall be added unto you. Fear not, little flock; for it is your Father's good pleasure to give you the kingdom."* (KJV)

In addition, Matthew 10:29-31:

> *"Are not two sparrows sold for a farthing? And*
> *one of them shall not fall on the ground without*
> *your Father. But the very hairs on your head*
> *are all numbered. Fear ye not therefore, ye are*
> *of more value than many sparrows."* (KJV)

The landlord of a rental property also requires a security deposit from the lessee to enter a binding contract on the property. The purpose of the security deposit is to ensure that the lessee will properly care for the property and not damage it in any way. Otherwise, the landlord, at the end of the lease, to compensate for any damage that has been inflicted on the property, will retain the normally refundable deposit. The lessee then forfeits the right to claim his deposit.

Jesus secured the deposit for our eternal dwelling place. John 3:16 tells us:

> *"God so loved the world, that He gave his*
> *only begotten Son, that whoever believed in*
> *him should not perish, but have everlasting*
> *life. For God sent not his son into the world to*
> *condemn the world; but that the world through*
> *him might be saved. He that believeth on Him*
> *is not condemned, but he that believeth not is*
> *condemned already."*(KJV)

You see, because God loved us so much, He made a deposit to secure our lives, through the death and resurrection of Jesus. If we claim the deposit by believing in Jesus, God will grant immortality in our eternal dwelling place. God has already paid the deposit for the permanently binding lease on our eternal lives.

CHAPTER 43

RISING FROM THE RUBBLE

This past weekend, my wife Donna and I decided to drive through the new campus of Bluegrass Community and Technical College at the site which once accommodated Eastern State Hospital, 627 West Fourth Street, in Lexington. History reveals that the hospital had perhaps as many as 12 different name changes between its inception as Fayette Hospital on September 10, 1817, and its relocation to 1350 Bull Lea Road on the University of Kentucky's Coldstream Research Campus in September 2013, where U. K. Health Care now manages the facilities. The actual name Eastern State Hospital was initially adopted more than 100 years ago in 1912. Nearly all the remaining names included the word *lunatic,* which we now condemn as extremely derogatory term, discriminatory, and politically incorrect. At one time, the campus, strategically located on the corner of Fourth Street and Newtown Pike, incorporated over 400 acres of mostly farmland.

Donna and I both had a curious interest in the

old hospital because we had watched as engineers and constructionists razed the old buildings, and the new Bluegrass Community and Technical College structure, like the Phoenix in Greek mythology, arose from the dust, rubble, and debris. The atmosphere also piqued our interest because my mother had spent nearly 30 years of her life as a chronic schizophrenic patient at the hospital, from December 1944 until the early 1970's. Here she had been locked in confined quarters for much of the time and undergone numerous shock treatments and experimental medical drugs and treatments. In addition, Donna served in a voluntary capacity for a couple of years after we left Concord Baptist church. Since she was no longer able to use her musical expertise in leading a church choir, she volunteered as accompanist for their weekly sing along sessions and the weekly chapel service.

Our informal and personal tour of the new facilities engendered nostalgic recollections as our senses consumed the aura of the restored Administration Building with its third floor Grand Ballroom. Donna had played the piano there, and my mother had walked the very halls of the former dormitories and administrative facilities. Perhaps she had walked through that same Grand Entrance, entered that same chapel, or perhaps even innocently absorbed the beauty of that very same third floor Grand Ballroom. The actual new BCTC main structure occupied the very sight where I visited my mother as a naïve wide eyed teenage boy over 55 years prior to that moment. The building where she had leaped from the second-floor balcony in an attempted suicide was now the site of a newly paved, well-lighted parking lot. The only remnants of the campus once teeming with doctors, white clad nurses, and seemingly aimless, insignificant, forgotten people now consisted only of the elegant Administration Building and one remaining dilapidated multi-gabled structure, perhaps scheduled for eventual demolition, that could have served as Mother's home for several years. How many lonely, despondent, troubled, and empty souls had meandered down those now forlorn hallways during Eastern State Hospital's nearly 200-year history? Many of them were buried in unnamed graves in the hospital's pauper cemetery.

Again, as I often am, in nostalgic moments, I was reminded of the meaningless and emptiness of "shadowy" lives of despair and hopelessness: empty people with empty eyes and empty souls searching for some semblance of hope in shattered memories and fragmented lives. Perhaps it was a more poignant experience for me because I knew my mother had been one of those "phantoms" in a society that had passed her by and had practically ignored her existence. Did she have importance in this life? Did she have an identity? Did anyone really care about her while she was there? Then, I became keenly aware that, because of God's abounding grace and love, the answer is a resounding, YES! She was not forgotten, and she was immensely valuable in the universe God has created. Even nameless, insignificant, unimportant people, buried in unnamed unknown gravesites are important in His eyes.

Romans 8:38-39: *For I am persuaded, that neither death nor life, nor angels, nor principalities, nor powers, nor things present, nor things to come, nor height, nor depth, nor any other creature, shall be able to separate us from the love of God, which is in Christ Jesus, our Lord.* (KJV)

Buildings come and go, we erect new structures, and we replace and forget old ones. However, do we really forget them? The new generation will have forgotten them in a few years, but Donna and I still remembered the old Eastern State Hospital nearly 200 years after it was constructed. Somebody will remember!

God remembers too! He was there, is still there, and will be there lovingly remembering my mother and others like her. Time passes, new structures come and go, new faces appear on the landscape, but God provides stability to the universe. My mother did matter and still does matters to somebody! She matters to me! She matters to God!

CHAPTER 44

DENMAX PROPERTIES

When I first met Elva Maxine Littrell in the summer of 2003, little did I suspect that this diminutive, petite 98-year-old million-dollar real estate agent would become another one of those "everyday ordinary saints" assigned by God to help me deepen my spirituality and navigate the future. She would impact my life in so many special ways: ways that I could never have deemed either imaginable or possible on this first encounter.

Maxine certainly did not have the physical appearance of a saint! Intense pain from chronic arthritis manifest itself in both a slight limp and a somewhat stooped curvature of her spine. In addition, she was not gifted with tremendous physical attraction, walked with her head slightly tilted forward, and was often clad in very "dated" clothing that I later discovered was probably purchased from the Goodwill Store. She generally manipulated her way through the streets of Lexington, depending on the year, in a somewhat banged up Honda Accord, Toyota Rav-4, or Nissan Rogue. It always amazed me that this lifetime member of The Million Dollar Club, an elite organization of the top producing realtors in Lexington, could park her banged up "used" vehicle next to a fellow member who drove a Cadillac, Lexus, or Mercedes and never bat an eye. Ironically, she probably had than more wealth than any of them and never expressed the desire to own a new car! She proudly claimed that her middle name was "Cheap" and was very careful never to reveal her wealth and her age.

My daughter Tracey, my wife Donna, and I had decided in that summer of 2003 that we would jointly seek the possibility of purchasing an investment property to augment our financial portfolio. I consulted a fellow church member who was a very successful investor and manager of several rental properties in the Winburn area of Lexington, and he informed me that he had purchased several of his properties with the assistance of his real estate agent, Maxine Littrell. We immediately contacted Maxine, and she graciously agreed to serve as our real estate agent. Little did we know that Maxine would not only become our real estate agent, but she would also become a very dear friend and often "adopted" member of our family for the next 17 years.   She   became another of those everyday ordinary saints.

In 2004, I received my real estate license, and Maxine I became very good friends and colleagues in the real estate business. Maxine was a real estate guru and amassed a real estate empire. At her death, she owned 28 rental properties (some duplexes) with 52 tenants. All properties, at her death, were worth several millions of dollars. In fact, at her death, she contributed $8,000,000 to the

Salvation Army. She never wanted anyone to know her age or how much money she had in her checking account. She never balanced her checkbook because she always said, "I know I have the money in there, so I don't need to balance the checkbook."

In 1918, she called me one evening from Nicholasville, where many of her properties were located, and told me she did not know where she was. She was lost. So, Donna and were getting ready to head out the door to try to find her, thinking where in the world could she be in Nicholasville. She called us back and said she now knew where she was. It was then that we recognized she had dementia and needed some help. She had no living relatives, so we "adopted" her for the next several years. It was then that she asked me to manage all her rental properties, which I more than glad to do, for the rest of her life. My wife and I happily welcomed her into our home to spend every Christmas and Thanksgiving at our house. I even opened her mail for her so that she could read it without forgetting where it was. My wife Donna even took her to get her hair cut and accompanied her on regular doctor's appointments. During one of those appointments, we discovered that she had advanced leukemia which eventually would take her away from us.

Upon her death, I, as a fellow real estate agent and property manager for her, was given the opportunity to sell all her real estate holdings. I saved every penny of my real estate commission from the sale of her properties and was given the opportunity to purchase seven of her duplexes in Nicholasville, KY. Consequently, my daughters Tracey and Amanda, my wife Donna, and I were able to establish

DenMax Properties, LLC. (A combination of Denny and Maxine). The value of our investments four years ago was around $1,500,000. I am almost a millionaire. However, Community Trust Bank has a pretty good investment in our company in the form of a mortgage.

CONCLUSION

OF SLEEP, PUZZLES, AND MISSING PIECES

Thornton Wilder's *Our Town*, Act I, scene ii (the stage manager speaks):

> "Now there are some things we all know, but we don't take'm out and look at e'm very often. We all know that something is eternal. And it ain't houses and it ain't names, and it ain't earth, and it ain't even the stars…everybody knows in their bones that something is eternal, and that something has to do with human beings. All the greatest people ever lived have been telling us that for five thousand years and yet you'd be surprised how people are always losing hold of it. There's something way down deep that's eternal about every human being."

As you are surely aware, there are times when sleep simply does not want to bring comfort to your somewhat restless spirit. Perhaps the worries of the day continue to haunt you. Perhaps the *David Letterman Show* does not quite serve to be a suitable sedative for the conclusion of the difficult day. Perhaps overwhelming grief over the death of a cherished loved one floods your soul. Perhaps *It's a Wonderful Life* elicits so many emotionally poignant feelings that you simply cannot quite "settle down." Your soul, in turn, becomes severely and deeply troubled. You teeter on the precipice of sinking into a quagmire of nostalgia or perhaps even deep despair.

I have sometimes even awakened in the middle of the night or in the wee early hours of the morning to a much too haunting memory, too intense and too teeming with melancholy thoughts to permit me the comfort of just a few more minutes of sleep. My lonely, troubled soul then seemed unable to discover any solution. I checked the alarm clock to verify that the chiming of the hallway clock was accurate. Sure enough, it was 3:00 a.m. in the morning. My mind wandered, and my imaginary conversation began. I addressed my thought to no one in particular. My silent inner voice was just lonely and desperate, sometimes addressed to the phantoms and shadows of the night as the occasional passing automobile headlights chased them across the bedroom ceiling.

> "I must be wide-awake for my 8:30 class in the morning. How can I teach *Julius Caesar* if I am exhausted and tired? Maybe I will not have to be very alert tomorrow.

238

Perhaps I can simply play the record of Act I. Wow, I also have that departmental meeting after school, followed by my countywide coordinator's meeting at the central office. How can I possibly make it through the entire day without help? Maybe a Tylenol would help. Then, there is church after that. I must be able to give the financial report with a clear mind; someone is always trying to trip me up on some trivial financial concern such as the deficit in the amount of money designated for the donut fund. God knows those donuts are certainly important! Maybe, if I close my eyes and concentrate, sleep will come."

Sometimes, however, sleep still does not come!

These times, amidst the solitary lonely blackness of the night, are often ones when my mind desperately turns to God. I offer up a small, feeble, desperate prayer.

"God, you have been so good to me, and I know you have more important things to deal with than my sleep. People are dying of debilitating cancers and excruciating heart attacks, and mothers' sons are being sacrificed on impersonal battlefields several thousand miles from home. But, please, please ease my restless mind! I am so exhausted! Yet, I cannot sleep. I don't

> fully understand why I am so disturbed.
> Perhaps I should have more faith in you?
> If so, please give me a stronger faith! Let
> me have some solace: just a few minutes
> of rest!"

Eventually sleep does come. The night changes to another day, the next day passes into oblivion, then changes to the next day, then the next, the next, and the next.

Sometimes, in sleepless moments such as these, my mind numbly settles into deep reflection about God and His heavenly compassion. I think about how He has ALWAYS cared for me, even when my mother was escorted off to Eastern State Hospital and even when both my brothers passed away and left me as the lone survivor much too soon. I wonder what He is really thinking about me. Maybe He is disappointed in the shallowness of my faith and my lack of total trust in Him.

On one such occasion, I imagined God as seated at some gigantic table, perhaps His heavenly coffee table, patiently searching for and putting in place the pieces of my life's puzzle.

Perhaps He diligently turns over the pieces and seeks out the edge pieces that will become the framework for the picture and begins assembling the panoramic view of my life. My old home place at Mom's house on Town Branch Road in Vanceburg will be one of the corner pieces, as will 990 Maywick Drive in Lexington, my home for over 50 years. One edge piece will certainly be the Herald Tremaine home on Haiti Road in Berea,

Ky. One corner piece must be the now indistinct organ factory on Scaffold Cane Road in Berea, where I had my first taste of true love. Danforth Chapel in the Draper Building on the campus of Berea College, where my wife and I wed over 59 years ago, will be the center point of the entire puzzle.

"Wait! Something is terribly wrong!" God proclaims, in a moment of disbelief and disappointment. "This puzzle cannot be completed. Some of the pieces are missing. I must find all the missing pieces."

"Oh, here in the folds of the couch is one. This represents the time when Denny "wandered away" from me and too independently "tried his wings" at Berea College back in 1962. Here is one piece under the coffee table: this shows the time when his faith in me faltered. I cannot believe he questioned my very existence after all I had done for him! Here is another strategic piece, under the newspaper on the end table. This captures the time when he doubted that I was walking with him during that big "church crisis" back in 1910. How could he have doubted I was with him the entire time? It is a little "chewed up" and mangled. In fact, those look like teeth marks on the edge. Ravage the cat has been at it again! I believe I can still use it, though. I must complete this puzzle! One human life is much too short and there are so many pieces! And I have so many other puzzles to solve!"

I can image God finally reaching for the final few pieces of my life, yet to be determined, and excitedly placing them in the only remaining slots.

"There. All finished. All the pieces are finally in place!"

Perhaps He will summon 10,000 angels to see if the finished work meets their approval. Perhaps He will instruct His heavenly angelic choir to loft to the heavenly rafters a few celebratory strains of the "Hallelujah Chorus." Perhaps He will simply frame the finished product and mount it on the walls of his Heavenly Chapel with all the others that are surely there.

However, there is another possible ending to the story of our lives.

"OH! NO! This is terrible! One piece is still missing!" God suddenly exclaims. "I am missing perhaps the most strategic piece, the very last one. This puzzle cannot be completed. How can this possibly be true? I have worked so hard on Denny, but he still does not believe in me or walk with me. This puzzle is certainly no good! It is only worthy of abandonment to Satan's trash heap of broken dreams, broken lives, and broken people. The puzzle must be destroyed! It is not worth keeping!"

How sad that we might approach the end of our lives with missing puzzle pieces!

I desperately desire that God will be able to find that last, most important piece of my life's puzzle. I surely want my life, regardless of sins, doubts, fears, and concerns over what might be the nature of the final pieces, to be a "keeper."

I want to be able to approach my "final sleep" as William Cullen Bryant envisioned in his ageless poem "Thanatopsis" ("a consideration of Death") over 150 years ago:

"So live, that when thy summons comes to join

The innumerable caravan which moves
To that mysterious realm where each shall
take
His chamber in the silent halls of death,
Thou go not, like the quarry-slave at night,
Scourged by his dungeon; but sustain'd
and soothed
By an unfaltering trust, approach thy grave,
Like one who wraps the drapery of his
couch
About him and lies down to pleasant
dreams."

With a secure and confident faith in God and with God's help, I will truly be able to welcome death as an old friend just as Bryant envisioned. I can wearily and sleepily accept the anticipated comfort of a soothing rest after a long, exhaustive, tumultuous journey. After all, tomorrow's dawn will arrive with a new sunrise and a fresh new day! Early tomorrow morning, the newspaper boy will still deliver the Lexington *Herald Leader* on schedule; Nikki, my neighbor across the street, will still cart off her children to daycare; and the yellow Fayette County school bus will still zoom down Maywick Drive on its way to Lafayette High School. Life will go on as usual for everyone else, but my life will begin a new, final, glorious, and eternal chapter.

In addition, I Corinthians 15:51-53: *Listen, I tell you a mystery: We shall not all sleep, but we will be changed—in a flash, in the twinkling of an eye, at the last trumpet. For the trumpet will sound, the dead will be raised imperishable, and we will be changed. For the perishable must clothe itself with the imperishable, and the mortal with immortality.* (NIV)

One of my favorite old hymns is "The longer I serve Him, the sweeter it grows." My life is very sweet!

Maybe I can now utter the words of Psalms 119 verse 11. "… How sweet are your words to my taste, sweeter than honey to my mouth! I gain understanding from your precepts; therefore, I hate every wrong path."